Houghton
Mifflin
Harcourt

PERFORMANCE
ASSESSMENT

12

Approaching Performance Assessments with Confidence

By Carol Jago

In order to get good at anything, you need to practice. Whether the goal is to improve your jump shot, level up in a video game, or make the cut in band tryouts, success requires repeated practice on the court, computer, and field. The same is true of reading and writing. The only way to get good at them is by reading and writing.

Malcolm Gladwell estimates in his book *Outliers* that mastering a skill requires about 10,000 hours of dedicated practice. He argues that individuals who are outstanding in their field have one thing in common—many, many hours of working at it. Gladwell claims that success is less dependent on innate talent than it is on practice. Now I'm pretty sure that I could put in 10,000 hours at a ballet studio and still be a terrible dancer, but I agree with Gladwell that, "Practice isn't the thing you do once you're good. It's the thing you do that makes you good."

Not just any kind of practice will help you master a skill, though. Effective practice needs to focus on improvement. That is why this series of reading and writing tasks begins with a model of the kind of reading and writing you are working towards, then takes you through practice exercises, and finally invites you to perform the skills you have practiced.

Once through the cycle is only the beginning. You will want to repeat the process many times over until close reading, supporting claims with evidence, and crafting a compelling essay is something you approach with confidence. Notice that I didn't say "with ease." I wish it were otherwise, but in my experience as a teacher and as an author, writing well is never easy.

The work is worth the effort. Like a star walking out on the stage, you put your trust in the hours you've invested in practice to result in thundering applause. To our work together!

Unit 1 Argumentative Essay
Pursuing a Dream

STEP 1 ANALYZE THE MODEL

Should you choose your career path based on future income or on other factors?

Read Source Materials

STEP 2 PRACTICE THE TASK

Is a college degree worth incurring significant debt?

Read Source Materials

Write an Argumentative Essay

STEP 3 PERFORM THE TASK

Is football too dangerous to be played in high school?

Read Source Materials

Write an Argumentative Essay

Is football too dangerous to be played in high school?

Unit 2 Informative Essay
Getting and Staying Healthy

STEP 1 ANALYZE THE MODEL

Are we mistreating our bodies?

Read Source Materials

STEP 2 PRACTICE THE TASK

How can people prevent diseases from spreading?

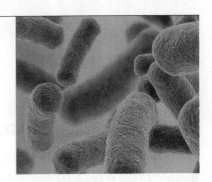

Read Source Materials

Write an Informative Esssay

How can people prevent diseases from spreading?

STEP 3 PERFORM THE TASK

How can we improve our health?

Read Source Materials

Write an Informative Essay

How can we improve our health?

Unit 3 Literary Analysis
Discoveries

STEP 1 ANALYZE THE MODEL

How can poetry help us rediscover the familiar?

Read Source Materials

STEP 2 PRACTICE THE TASK

What effects do past cultures have on literature?

Read Source Materials

Write a Literary Analysis

STEP 3 PERFORM THE TASK

How does literature help us answer our questions about life?

Read Source Materials

Write a Literary Analysis

Unit 4 Mixed Practice
On Your Own

© Houghton Mifflin Harcourt Publishing Company

Pursuing a Dream

Argumentative Essay

STEP 1

ANALYZE THE MODEL

Evaluate an argumentative essay that claims that potential future earnings should not be the only factor when considering careers.

STEP 2

PRACTICE THE TASK

Write an argumentative essay that takes a position on whether college is worth the cost of incurring debt.

STEP 3

PERFORM THE TASK

Write an argumentative essay that answers the question: Is high school football too dangerous?

Disagreement is a very human trait. Interacting with others—friends, neighbors, relatives, strangers—sometimes can lead to disagreements. Arguing your reasons for your stance on an issue and explaining your point of view face to face can be challenging. The argumentative essay, on the other hand, provides a platform for more formally constructed argument.

IN THIS UNIT, you will learn how to write an argumentative essay that is based on your close reading and analysis of several relevant sources. You will learn a step-by-step approach to stating a claim, and then organizing your essay to support your claim in a clear and logical way.

ANALYZE THE MODEL

Should you choose your career path based on future income or on other factors?

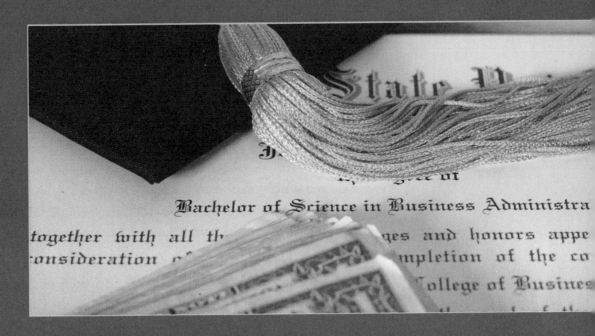

You will read:

▶ **A RADIO INTERVIEW**
Choosing a Career

▶ **AN INFORMATIONAL ARTICLE**
What Makes Work Satisfying?

You will analyze:

▶ **A STUDENT MODEL**
Money Isn't Everything

Source Materials for Step 1

The texts on these two pages were used by Mr. O'Donnell's student, Lidia George, as sources for her essay "Money Isn't Everything." As you read, make notes in the side columns and underline information that you find useful.

Source 1: Radio Interview

NOTES

Choosing a Career

WTBU College Radio's Tasheeka Matthews surveys four students on their career goals and decision-making process.

WTBU: Deena, you're pre-med. Are you up for all the years of training and hard work ahead?

Deena: Yes, I am. I know they will be hard, but the investment will pay off. I'm looking forward to a career in medicine with a high income, and lots of challenge and responsibility every day. I really like to be in charge, so being a doctor is a good choice for me.

Rob: Well, that's great for you, but I really wouldn't want all that debt and so many more years of school. I love medicine, but I don't need the stress of being a doctor—so I'm going for my RN. There's great job security, and I'll be able to find work no matter where I live.

Rasheed: What matters most for me is the work environment. I'm training to be a web designer and computer programmer. I don't like being told what to do or telling people what to do—I like working with others. So something nontraditional and nerdy but creative like web design is perfect for me.

Stephanie: I don't really know 100% what I want to do yet, but I want to work with young children. I'm getting my elementary teaching certificate, but at some point I may go back and do something more specific, like counseling or speech therapy. Young children make me laugh, and laughing is the key to everything for me. I know the salary won't be high, but if I'm happy everyday and helping others, who cares?

WTBU: I'm impressed with all of your plans and your commitment. Best of luck to all of you!

1. Analyze   2. Practice   3. Perform

Source 2: Informational Article

What Makes Work Satisfying?

Findings from the Committee for Job Satisfaction in America

NOTES

Job satisfaction depends on a variety of factors. For example, the occupation of singer appears high on many job satisfaction lists, but if you want to be a singer, you should know that, unless you make it big, you won't make a lot of money. Why, then, might singers be among the people most satisfied with their job? They do not work standard hours, for one. They can tap into creative outlets. They may be self-employed, and thus in control of their finances. Every performance is different, and they may work in different venues. A singer who is satisfied with her job may not consider salary a top priority. Being a singer does not necessarily require a lot of schooling, so people in this profession may not have to contend with school loans.

Those who work in the medical field, including physical therapists, are also very satisfied with their jobs. This might be due to the fact that they will have employment opportunities in any state, because their skills translate to hospitals or private clinics across the nation. Physical therapists make a good salary. They help people recover after trauma or illness, which can be rewarding. They may have incurred student loans, but their salary will cover those expenses.

It might surprise you to know that firefighters rank highly on job satisfaction lists. Although firefighters do not make a lot of money and are constantly exposed to dangerous circumstances, they are satisfied with their jobs. One draw is the challenge the job provides: Firefighters rescue people, animals, and forests from fires. Their actions save lives and homes. Firefighters spend much of their time in fire stations together, where they can form close bonds with one another. This reinforces their shared responsibility of keeping people from harm.

Discuss and Decide

You have read and analyzed two sources about careers. Without going any further, discuss the question: Would you choose your career path based on future income or on other factors?

Analyze a Student Model for Step 1

Read Lidia's argumentative essay closely. The red side notes are the comments from her teacher, Mr. O'Donnell.

Lidia George
Mr. O'Donnell
English 12
September 21

Money
Isn't Everything

Your claim is clearly stated.

Do I want to be rich? Of course. I'd be crazy or a liar if I said I didn't. But I also want to be happy, and there's more to finding happiness than making a pile of money.

Money can buy vacations and cars and houses—and those things are great—but it can't buy the feeling of being excited about what you are doing everyday. It can't buy pride in a job well done, or gratification when work helps others or moves a project forward. It can't buy daily satisfaction and contentment.

Loving what you do is a valid reason.

Opposing claim is stated and answered clearly.

Some people tell themselves that if they have money, they will be able to do lots of fun things on weekends and live in a way that makes them happy. That is true to a certain extent. But over a whole lifetime, the average person spends around 90,000 hours at work. That's a lot! It makes sense to spend those hours doing something you enjoy.

There are lots of things you can't control when choosing a career path, but you should at least think hard about what is important to you and try to rank those things in order of importance. Which of the following factors, for example, would be the most important for you when deciding on a job?

- **Job security:** Do you care where you work? Are you ready to be sent anywhere, or do you prefer to stay near friends and family?

- **Job security:** Are you looking for a job for life, or are you ready and willing to go for something shorter-term but possibly more exciting?

- **Work environment:** Can you handle stress and competition, or do you need a supportive gang of coworkers around you?

- **Personal values:** Do you need your job to be a direct expression of your personal commitment to make the world a better place? Or can you save your good deeds for the weekends?

- **Work hours:** Are you okay with a job that never stops (long weeks and little vacation time), or is it important to you to have plenty of time off for friends and family?

By all means put income into the mix when deciding which career path is best for you, but please, don't let the dollar signs make the decision on their own.

Your use of a bulleted list is creative and organized.

You restate your claim creatively.

Discuss and Decide

Did Lidia's essay convince you that money is not the most important thing to consider when choosing a career and why? Cite evidence in your response.

Terminology of Argumentative Texts

Read each term and explanation. Then look back at Lidia George's argumentative essay and find an example to complete the chart.

Term	Explanation	Example from Lidia's Essay
audience	The **audience** for your argument is a group of people that you want to convince. As you develop your argument, consider your audience's knowledge level and concerns.	
purpose	The **purpose** for writing an argument is to sway the audience. Your purpose should be clear, whether it is to persuade your audience to agree with your claim, or to motivate your audience to take some action.	
precise claim	A **precise claim** confidently states your viewpoint. Remember that you must be able to support your claim with reasons and evidence, and that you must distinguish your claim from opposing claims.	
reason	A **reason** is a statement that supports your claim. (You should have more than one reason.) Note that you will need to supply evidence for each reason you state.	
opposing claim	An **opposing claim**, or **counterclaim**, shares the point of view of people who do not agree with your claim. Opposing claims must be presented fairly with evidence.	

Is a college degree worth incurring significant debt?

You will read:

▶ **A CONSUMER REPORT**
Shopping for a College Loan? Don't Get Taken!

▶ **A DATA ANALYSIS**

▶ **A LIST**
10 Best Jobs You Can Get Without a College Degree

▶ **A FINANCIAL ADVICE COLUMN**

You will write:

▶ **AN ARGUMENTATIVE ESSAY**
Is a college degree worth incurring significant debt?

Source Materials for Step 2

Analyze the consumer report, data analysis, list, and column. Think about the information, including the data contained in the sources. Annotate the sources with notes that help you decide where you stand on the issue: Is a college degree worth incurring significant debt?

Source 1: Consumer Report

Shopping for a College Loan?
Don't Get Taken!

Have you ever seen an ad for student loans that looks something like this? Does it seem too good to be true? Well, that's because it probably is. Students today feel pressure to get a degree, or even two. They know that education is important. But the question is, at what cost?

College tuition rates keep going up, and students are taking out bigger and bigger loans. It's far too easy to get $50,000, $75,000, even $100,000 regardless of likely or possible future earnings. If the student drops out, graduates but is either unemployed or underemployed, or can find only low-paying work, it may be next to impossible to pay back the loans. After all, you can't squeeze blood from a stone.

Easy College Loans!

Available to full-time, part-time, and continuing-education students.
In today's world, everyone needs a college degree.
No payments while at school.
Easy credit terms and payment options.
Create a brighter future. Invest in yourself today!

Private lenders who lure customers with ads like this are not trying to help you get your education. They are looking to make money. High-interest loans are a good deal for the lender, but not for the student who will start out in life saddled with an impossibly heavy debt burden that may take 20 years or more to pay off. Think twice before getting in over your head with debt that may last a lifetime!

Close Read

Does this author think that a college education is valuable? Cite text evidence in support of that viewpoint.

_____

_____

1. Analyze   2. Practice   3. Perform

Source 2: Data Analysis

How Much Income Can I Expect to Earn With My Degree?

This chart represents the total income Americans expect to earn in their lifetimes. The sections compare what percentage of total income one could expect to earn, depending on educational level attained by 2008.

Note: Percentages have been rounded up.

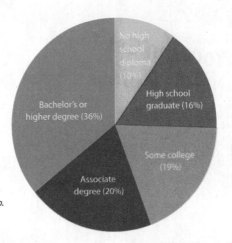

Median Annual Earnings by Age and Educational Attainment

(Full-time, year-round workers)

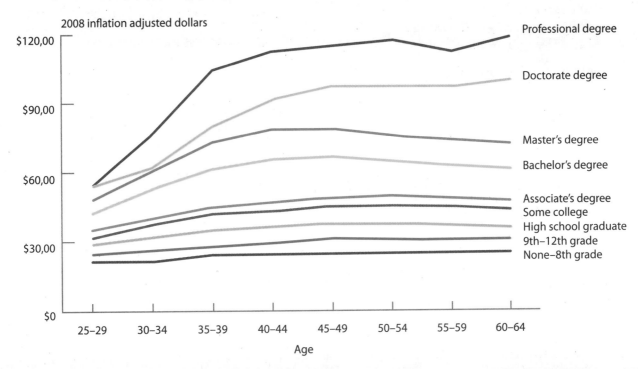

Source: U.S. Census Bureau, American Community Survey, 2006–2008.

Source 3: List

10 Best Jobs You Can Get Without a College Degree

10 **MANUFACTURING SALES REPS**
Median salary: $52,440 (U.S. median: $41,444)
Projected job growth, 2010–2020: 16%
(Average: 14%)
Projected new jobs by 2020: 223,400

9 **TELECOMMUNICATIONS EQUIPMENT INSTALLERS**
Median salary: $54,710
Projected job growth, 2010–2020: 15%
Projected new jobs by 2020: 28,400

8 **INSURANCE SALES AGENTS**
Median salary: $46,770
Projected job growth, 2010–2020: 22%
Projected new jobs by 2020: 90,200

7 **CONSTRUCTION & BUILDING INSPECTORS**
Median salary: $52,360
Projected job growth, 2010–2020: 18%
Projected new jobs by 2020: 18,400

6 **PLUMBERS, PIPEFITTERS, & STEAMFITTERS**
Median salary: $46,660
Projected job growth, 2010–2020: 26%
Projected new jobs by 2020: 107,600

5 **DRY WALL TAPERS**
Median salary: $45,490
Projected job growth, 2010–2020: 35%
Projected new jobs by 2020: 8,000

4 **ELECTRICIANS**
Median salary: $48,250
Projected job growth, 2010–2020: 23%
Projected new jobs by 2020: 133,700

3 **COMMERCIAL PILOTS**
Median salary: $67,500
Projected job growth, 2010–2020: 21%
Projected new jobs by 2020: 6,900

2 **BRICKMASONS & BLOCKMASONS**
Median salary: $46,930
Projected job growth, 2010–2020: 41%
Projected new jobs by 2020: 36,100

1 **PILE-DRIVER OPERATORS**
Median salary: $47,860
Projected job growth, 2010–2020: 36%
Projected new jobs by 2020: 1,500

Discuss and Decide

1. Compare the charts in Source 2. What effect does a college degree have on a person's earning potential?

2. Compare the data presented in Sources 2 and 3. What conclusions can you draw from the data? What inconsistencies do you find, if any?

1. Analyze   2. Practice   3. Perform

Source 4: Financial Advice Column

Dear Money-Pro:

Everyone says I should go to college, but it is so expensive. I find it hard to believe it is really worth all that money. Wouldn't it make more sense to just try to find a job right after I finish high school?

Sincerely,
Skeptical

Dear Skeptical:

I know that college is expensive and time consuming, but, if you think you can graduate, the investment of time and money is likely (but not guaranteed) to be worthwhile. Consider these facts:

— Lifetime earnings for a college grad are substantially higher than the earnings of someone without a college degree, even when you deduct all the money you would have made if you had been working full-time and the costs of student loans. Plus, this earnings gap is getting wider.

— College graduates are more likely to find job opportunities and be employed. They are also less likely to lose their jobs in a recession.

— College grads are happier in their jobs. Maybe that's because they are more likely to get health care coverage and other benefits through their work.

— Getting a degree isn't only good for you, it's good for your community and your family as well: College grads pay more taxes and are more engaged citizens and parents. They participate in more educational activities in the family, so their children arrive at school better prepared than the children of those without a college degree.

Of course, it doesn't make sense to take out loans for college if you are likely to drop out. Even without a diploma, that money has to be repaid, with interest.

Sincerely,
Money-Pro

Close Read

What facts in Source 2 support Money-Pro's claims?

_____

_____

Respond to Questions on Step 2 Sources

These questions will help you analyze the texts you've read. Use your notes and refer to the sources in order to answer the questions. Your answers to these questions will help you write your essay.

1 Evaluate the sources. Is the evidence from one source more credible than the evidence from another source? When you evaluate the credibility of a source, examine the expertise of the author and/or the organization responsible for the information. Record your reasons in the chart.

Source	Credible?	Reasons
Consumer Report Shopping for a College Loan? Don't Get Taken!		
Data Analysis		
List 10 Best Jobs You Can Get Without a College Degree		
Financial Advice Column		

2 **Prose Constructed-Response** The sources you have read each take a position on incurring debt for education. Analyze the strengths of the arguments made in at least two of the sources. Remember to use textual evidence to support your ideas.

_____

_____

3 **Prose Constructed-Response** Using information from at least two of the sources you read, summarize an argument you would use on a younger relative if she told you that college is a waste of money and time. Remember to use textual evidence to support your ideas.

_____

_____

Types of Evidence

Every reason you offer to support the central claim of your argument must be upheld by evidence. It is useful to think ahead about evidence when you are preparing to write an argument. If there is no evidence to support your claim, you will need to revise your claim. The evidence you provide must be relevant, or related to your claim. It must also be sufficient. Sufficient evidence is both clear and varied.

Use this chart to help you vary the types of evidence you provide to support your reasons.

Types of Evidence	What Does It Look Like?
Anecdotes: personal examples or stories that illustrate a point	**Consumer Report** "Students today feel pressure to get a degree . . ."
Commonly accepted beliefs: ideas that most people share	**Financial Advice Column** ". . . college is expensive . . ."
Examples: specific instances or illustrations of a general idea	**List** Commercial pilots earn a median annual salary of $67,500.
Expert opinion: statement made by an authority on the subject	**Data Analysis** Someone with an associate degree earns twice as much during their lifetime as someone with no high school diploma.
Facts: statements that can be proven true, such as statistics or other numerical information	**Data Analysis** Someone who has attended college without receiving a degree earns about as much over their lifetime as someone who has an associate degree.

Write an argumentative essay to answer the question: Is a college degree worth incurring significant debt?

Planning and Prewriting

Before you draft your essay, complete some important planning steps

Claim ⇒ Reasons ⇒ Evidence

 You may prefer to do your planning on your computer.

Make a Precise Claim

1. Is a college degree worth incurring significant debt?

yes ☐   no ☐

2. Review the evidence on pages 10–13. Do the sources support your position?

yes ☐   no ☐

3. If you answered *no* to Question 2, you can either change your position or do additional research to find supporting evidence.

4. State your claim. It should be precise. It should contain the issue and your position on the issue.

> **Issue:** College degrees incur significant debt.
>
> **Your position on the issue:** _____
>
> **Your precise claim:** _____

State Reasons

Next gather support for your claim. Identify several valid reasons that justify your position.

Reason 1	Reason 2	Reason 3

Find Evidence

You have identified reasons that support your claim. Summarize your reasons in the chart below. Then complete the chart by identifying evidence that supports your reasons.

Relevant Evidence: The evidence you plan to use must be *relevant* to your argument. That is, it should directly and factually support your position.

Sufficient Evidence: Additionally, your evidence must be *sufficient* to make your case. That is, you need to supply enough evidence to convince others.

Short Summary of Reasons	Evidence
Reason 1	Relevant? _____ Sufficient? _____
Reason 2	Relevant? _____ Sufficient? _____
Reason 3	Relevant? _____ Sufficient? _____

Finalize Your Plan

Whether you are writing your essay at home or working in a timed situation at school, it is important to have a plan. You will save time and create a more organized, logical essay by planning the structure before you start writing.

Use your responses on pages 18–19, as well as your close reading notes, to complete the graphic organizer.

▶ Think about how you will grab your reader's attention with an interesting fact or anecdote.

▶ Identify the issue and your position.

▶ State your precise claim.
▶ List the likely opposing claim and how you will counter it.

▶ Restate your claim.

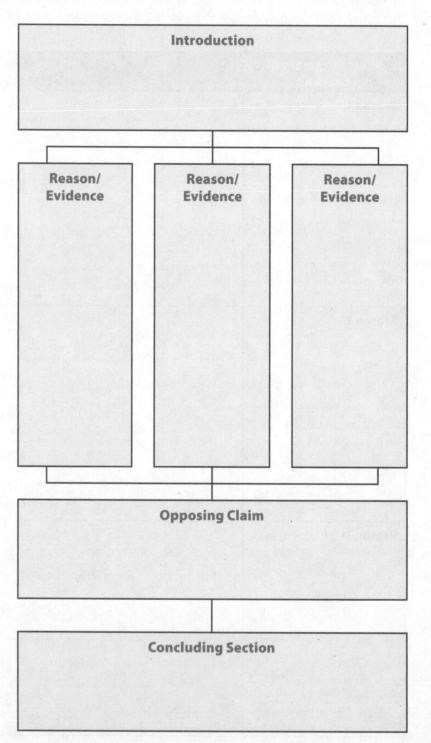

Introduction

Reason/Evidence	Reason/Evidence	Reason/Evidence

Opposing Claim

Concluding Section

Draft Your Essay

As you write, think about:

▶ **Audience:** Your teacher

▶ **Purpose:** Demonstrate your understanding of the specific requirements of an argumentative essay

▶ **Style:** Use a formal and objective tone that isn't defensive.

▶ **Transitions:** Use words, such as *furthermore* or *another reason*, to create cohesion or flow.

Revise

Use the checklist below to guide your analysis.

Revision Checklist: Self Evaluation

 If you drafted your essay on the computer, you may wish to print it out so that you can evaluate it more easily.

Ask Yourself	Tips	Revision Strategies
1. Does the introduction grab the audience's attention and include a precise claim?	Draw a wavy line under the attention-grabbing text. Bracket the claim.	Add an attention grabber. Add a claim or rework the existing one to make it more precise.
2. Do at least two valid reasons support the claim? Is each reason supported by relevant and sufficient evidence?	Underline each reason. Circle each piece of evidence, and draw an arrow to the reason it supports.	Add reasons or revise existing ones to make them more valid. Add relevant evidence to ensure that your support is sufficient.
3. Do transitions create cohesion and link related parts of the argument?	Put a star next to each transition.	Add words, phrases, or clauses to connect related ideas that lack transitions.
4. Are the reasons in the order that is most persuasive?	Number the reasons in the margin, ranking them by their strength and effectiveness.	Rearrange the reasons into a more logical order, such as order of importance.
5. Are opposing claims fairly acknowledged and refuted?	Put a plus sign by any sentence that addresses an opposing claim.	Add sentences that identify and address those opposing claims.
6. Does the concluding section restate the claim?	Put a box around the restatement of your claim.	Add a sentence that restates your claim.

Revision Checklist: Peer Review

Exchange your essay with a classmate, or read it aloud to your partner. As you read and comment on your classmate's essay, focus on logic, organization, and evidence—not on whether you agree with the author's claim. Help each other identify parts of the draft that need strengthening, reworking, or a new approach.

What To Look For	Notes for My Partner
1. Does the introduction grab the audience's attention and include a precise claim?	
2. Do at least two valid reasons support the claim? Is each reason supported by relevant and sufficient evidence?	
3. Do transitions create cohesion and link related parts of the argument?	
4. Are the reasons in the order that is most persuasive?	
5. Are opposing claims fairly acknowledged and refuted?	
6. Does the concluding section restate the claim?	

Edit

 Edit your essay to correct spelling, grammar, and punctuation errors.

Is football too dangerous to be played in high school?

You will read:

▶ **A SCIENCE ARTICLE**
How Dangerous Is High School Football?

▶ **A NEWS ARTICLE**
Hard Knocks

▶ **AN INFORMATIONAL ARTICLE**
With Proper Oversight, Youth Football Is Safe

You will write:

▶ **AN ARGUMENTATIVE ESSAY**
Is football too dangerous to be played in high school?

How Dangerous Is High School Football?

from Nationwide Children's Hospital

AS YOU READ *Look for evidence that supports your position on the dangers of high school football, or inspires you to change your position.*

NOTES

Football, one of the most popular sports in the United States, is also the leading cause of sports-related injuries. During the 2005-06 season, high school football players sustained more than half a million injuries nationally. A study conducted by researchers in the Center for Injury Research and Policy (CIRP) at Columbus Children's Hospital, is the first to compare injuries among high school and collegiate football players using a nationally representative sample.

According to the study, published in the August 2007 issue of *The American Journal of Sports Medicine*, four out of every 1,000 high school football exposures resulted in an injury, while eight out of every 1,000 collegiate football exposures resulted in an injury. Although National Collegiate Athletic Association (NCAA) football players were twice as likely to sustain an injury as high school football players, high school football players sustained a greater proportion of season-ending injuries, fractures and concussions compared to collegiate football players.

"While football does have a high rate of injuries, injuries don't have to be just part of the game," said Christy Collins, MA, research associate in CIRP at Children's Hospital and co-author of the study. "There are ways to reduce the number and severity of football injuries through targeted interventions. Because we observed high levels of ankle and knee injuries, we recommend increased conditioning of ankles and knees and rule changes aimed at protecting these vulnerable body sites. As most of the injuries to these regions were due to ligament sprains, targeted stretching exercises may also be beneficial."

Running plays were the leading cause of injury in both high school and collegiate football, and in high school they accounted for the majority of season-ending injuries and concussions. Positions with the greatest risk of injury were running backs and linebackers.

30   Dawn Comstock, PhD, CIRP principal investigator, faculty member at Ohio State University College of Medicine and co-author of the study, suggested, "Additional instruction on appropriate tackling and blocking techniques as well as position-specific conditioning may help reduce the risk of injury during running plays."

    "Further research is required to identify those players most likely to be injured and examine what types of targeted efforts might prevent those injuries," said Collins. "Also, there is a need for further analysis in the difference between high school and collegiate-level athletes and why high school players had greater proportions of the more severe injuries."

    Data for the study were collected from the 2005-06 U.S. High
40 School Sports-Related Injury Surveillance Study and the 2005-06 NCAA Injury Surveillance System. Collected from this data were the injuries from 100 high school football teams and 55 NCAA football teams.

NOTES

Close Read

What advice does the article give on reducing the number of injuries to high school football players? Cite text evidence in your response.

_____

_____

_____

Hard Knocks

by Alan Schwarz   from *The New York Times Upfront*

AS YOU READ *Pay attention to the evidence about head injuries. Jot down comments or questions about the text in the side margins.*

NOTES

Head injuries among football players are rising and the after-effects are more serious than previously thought.

Is football just too dangerous?

Owen Thomas started playing football when he was 9 years old. From the beginning, he enjoyed the rough-and-tumble of the game.

"He loved to go into practice and hit really hard," recalls his mother, Kathy Brearley.

Over time, those hits added up and appear to have taken a terrible toll. In April, Thomas—a junior at the University of Pennsylvania and a lineman on its football team—took his own life. The autopsy showed that his brain was in the early stages of chronic traumatic
10   encephalopathy, more commonly known as C.T.E.

C.T.E. is a head-trauma-induced disease linked to depression, impulse-control problems, memory loss, and dementia. More than 20 deceased N.F.L. players have been found to have had C.T.E.

But its discovery in a 21-year-old who had never even been diagnosed with a concussion raises big questions about the dangers of football, especially for the 1.4 million high school students and 3 million younger kids who play.

If this debilitating brain disease can be caused by repeated hits to the head that don't rise to the level of a concussion—an intrinsic
20   part of football at every level—is it even possible to make the game safe? In general, there's an increasing awareness about the dangers of concussions—especially for younger players whose brains are still developing.

'Brain Damage, Pure and Simple'

Because football's gladiator culture encourages playing through pain and taking a hit for the team, many teens don't want to risk being put on the sidelines by telling their coaches when they think they might have a concussion.

Concussions are more dangerous for teenagers because, studies show, their brain tissue is less developed than adults' and more easily damaged. High school players also typically receive less expert medical care than college or pro players, or none at all.

There's also the question of helmets. Many young players use old safety gear that's been passed down long past its prime. And even new helmets are designed to prevent only skull fractures, not concussions.

So what can be done to make football safer? Improving helmet technology is a good place to start. Better still, doctors say, coaches need to do a better job of making sure any player with a head injury stays off the field long enough for the injury to fully heal.

But medical experts say the most important change is to reduce the overall number of hits to the head—in practice as well as in games. Football is probably the most practice-intensive team sport—one recent study found that a college football player participates in an average of 12 practices for every game played—and players often sustain hits during practice.

"We can, and we must, develop brain trauma guidelines similar to the pitch-count regulations now used in Little League Baseball," says Dr. Robert Cantu, a professor of neurosurgery at Boston University. "We count the pitches of every baseball player to ensure a small number do not develop shoulder and elbow problems—and yet we don't count how often children get hit in the head playing football."

In an effort to prevent some of the more harmful hits, the N.F.L. has started to crack down on players who violate existing rules against unnecessary or intentional hits, fining them and threatening to suspend them. The N.F.L. is also considering ways to change the frequency and structure of its practices to reduce head trauma. Those who love the game are hopeful that all these changes will make a difference.

"I definitely think the game can be made safer," says Michael Oriard, a former N.F.L. player who has written several books about the game. "But can it be made safe enough? I'm not so sure."

Discuss and Decide

Which solution is the N.F.L. considering to prevent harmful injuries? Would this help high school players?

With Proper Oversight, Youth Football Is Safe

by Terrence Holder

AS YOU READ *Pay attention to details about making football safer. Jot down comments or questions about the text in the side margins.*

NOTES

Concussions and their long-term effects on NFL players have raised concerns about the effects that head injuries may have on teen players. There is evidence that younger athletes, whose brains are still developing, may be even more vulnerable to brain injuries than adult athletes. However, there are many new changes already put in motion in the youth game that will ensure that the dangers of head injuries and other significant injuries keep the game safe for our youth.

Many of the changes in youth football come from the recommendations of sports medicine experts. Mark Lovell, who founded the University of Pittsburgh Medical Center's Sports Medicine Concussion Program, recommends several changes to limit concussions:

1. Have doctors and trainers on the field who understand the injury.
2. Use standardized concussion tests to determine if an injured player is ready to return.
3. Ease injured athletes back into play gradually.
4. Monitor injured players long term.

Although there is no national body that oversees youth football, Pop Warner—which is similar in its position in youth sports to the Little League baseball—had 250,000 young football players aged 5–16 in 2010. A 1998 study showed that the incidence of injuries, and particularly serious injuries among Pop Warner football is low—significantly lower than football players at the college and professional levels.

1. Analyze   2. Practice   3. Perform

Part of the safety program that Pop Warner oversees is a schema for competition that has athletes playing against other athletes of similar age and size. This minimizes situations where larger athletes inflict punishing blows on smaller ones. Players are also taught not to use their helmets to make a tackle.

30 Pop Warner had also enacted rule changes in 2012 to prevent concussions. Coaches are being directed away from the old-school idea that practice should include a great deal of contact.

The rule changes include ones that limit contact in practices:

1. No full-speed head-on blocking or tackling drills in practice, and no intentional head-to-head contact.
2. The amount of contact at each practice is limited to 1/3 of practice time.

In addition, any head or neck injury to a player requires a doctor's note for the athlete to return to play. Pop Warner has also set limits on how long a player can stay in a game. The organization is pondering a
40 future requirement for annual brain scans for athletes to identify young athletes who may be at risk for brain injuries.

There are other safety measures that make an important difference. Modern equipment that provides greater protection for college level players, is also available for younger players. Training methods that involve sustained conditioning prior to the start of contact help athletes avoid muscle strains and ligament tears.

There is no question that the threat of concussion has raised awareness of the danger of football injuries. But with proper coaching, conditioning, equipment, and limitations on contact, football can be
50 safer.

Close Read

Who is Mark Lovell and why is he quoted in this article? Cite text evidence in your response.

_____

_____

_____

Respond to Questions on Step 3 Sources

These questions will help analyze the sources you've read. Use your notes and refer back to the sources to answer the questions. Your answers to these questions will help you write your essay.

1 Is the evidence from one source more credible than the evidence from another source? When you evaluate the credibility of a source, examine the expertise of the author and/or the organization responsible for the information. Record your reasons.

Source	Credible?	Reasons
Science Article How Dangerous Is High School Football?		
News Article Hard Knocks		
Informational Article With Proper Oversight, Youth Football Is Safe		

2 **Prose Constructed-Response** What point about playing football is made in all three sources? Why is this point important to address when making an informed decision about the dangers of playing football? Cite text evidence to support your answer.

_____

_____

_____

3 **Prose Constructed-Response** Does the evidence in " How Dangerous Is High School Football?" support or contradict the evidence in "Hard Knocks"? Cite text evidence to support your answer.

_____

_____

Part 2: Write

Plan

Use the graphic organizer to help you outline the structure of your argumentative essay.

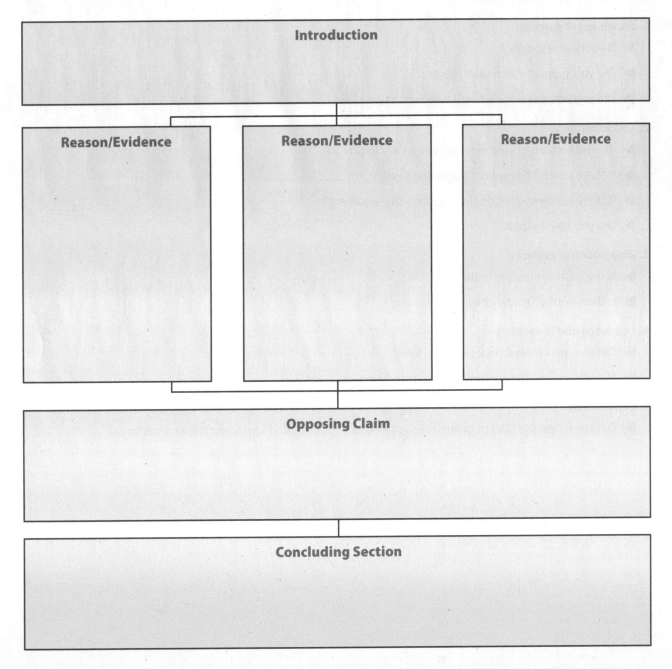

Draft

 Use your notes and completed graphic organizer to write a first draft of your argumentative essay.

Revise and Edit

 Look back over your essay and compare it to the Evaluation Criteria. Revise your essay and edit it to correct spelling, grammar, and punctuation errors.

Evaluation Criteria

Your teacher will be looking for:

1. *Statement of purpose*

 ▶ Is your claim specific?

 ▶ Did you support it with valid reasons?

 ▶ Did you anticipate and address opposing claims fairly?

2. *Organization*

 ▶ Are the sections of your essay organized in a logical way?

 ▶ Is there a smooth flow from beginning to end?

 ▶ Is there a clear conclusion that supports the argument?

 ▶ Did you stay on topic?

3. *Elaboration of evidence*

 ▶ Is the evidence relative to the topic?

 ▶ Is there enough evidence to be convincing?

4. *Language and Vocabulary*

 ▶ Did you use a formal, noncombative tone?

 ▶ Did you use vocabulary familiar to your audience?

5. *Conventions*

 ▶ Did you follow the rules of grammar usage as well as punctuation, capitalization, and spelling?

Getting and Staying Healthy

Informative Essay

STEP 1

ANALYZE THE MODEL

Read an informational article on obesity and analyze a student's informative essay on unhealthy diets.

STEP 2

PRACTICE THE TASK

Write an informative essay on disease prevention.

STEP 3

PERFORM THE TASK

Write an informative essay on how our daily activities impact our health.

Informative writing, or expository writing, informs and explains. Informational writing works with facts and can be used to evaluate the effects of a weight loss supplement, explain how the newest technological gadget works, or keep people up to date on a developing story overseas. Successful informational essays examine and clearly convey ideas and information.

The texts you will read in this unit explore current issues in public health and ways to get and stay healthy.

IN THIS UNIT, you will analyze information from nonfiction articles, essays, blogs, and a press release. You will evaluate and synthesize the information presented in these texts. Then you will use what you have learned to write informative essays of your own.

Are we mistreating our bodies?

You will read:

▶ **TWO INFORMATIONAL ARTICLES**
Organization First

Americans Are Eating Fewer Calories, So Why Are We Still Obese?

You will analyze:

▶ **A STUDENT MODEL**
Sugar, Salt, Fat: How to Deal with This Public Health Triple Threat

Source Materials for Step 1

Ms. Steiner's students read the article below to help them learn how to write an informative essay. Then, they read an informational article on obesity.

Organization First

A good informative essay explains its topic clearly and logically. Good expository writing often takes information from a variety of sources and synthesizes it into a concise piece for the reader— the writer has read a variety of sources, reviewed them, and then explained them, so you don't have to!

The first step in writing an informative essay is gathering information from a variety of sources. Then, you must integrate this text selectively, choosing only the most relevant information for your essay. As you evaluate your sources, make note of the most important idea in each. Then, develop your main idea. What do you want your reader to know?

Whenever you put together facts, ideas, and details from different sources to form your own understanding of a topic, you are synthesizing, or integrating, information. You can usually gain deeper insight into a topic by synthesizing from several sources than by just reading one source.

Once you have located credible sources, use a graphic organizer to take in-depth notes. Jot down facts, details, examples, statistics, and other evidence relevant to your research question. At the same time, look for opportunities to synthesize information—to draw insightful conclusions about your topic using a variety of sources and your own prior knowledge.

Source	Important Details and Ideas	Questions
"The Lungs that Breathe for Us" lecture	• transport oxygen from outside of the body into the bloodstream	What needs to happen for oxygen to get to the lungs?
"The Circulatory System" informational pamphlet	• sends nutrients and oxygen to and from cells in the body • cardiovascular and lymphatic system handle distribution of blood	How does the oxygen from the lungs get distributed?

Once you have decided on your topic, proceed to organize your essay. You will communicate your ideas more efficiently by sharing the facts, definitions, details, and examples you have researched in a well-planned essay. Some text structures may be more appropriate for your topic than others.

© Houghton Mifflin Harcourt Publishing Company

NOTES

- If you have several strong points to make, each of which is supported by examples and details, use a main-idea-and-detail structure. This structure will help you present all of your information in a way that makes logical sense.

- If you want to show how you topic changed over time, use a chronological structure. This organization is an easy way to trace the evolution of your topic.

- If how things are alike and different is an important part of your controlling idea, use a compare-and-contrast structure. This will help you organize your information in a way that will clarify your points.

- If there are multiple factors that contribute to one event, or a single event that resulted in multiple outcomes, use a cause-and-effect structure. Showing the causal relationship will clarify the interconnectedness of events.

Now you can start writing. Use a framework for writing to help you focus and manage information and ideas.

Framework for an Informative Essay

Introduction
Hook your reader's interest and clearly identify your subject. Make your topic and main point clear.

Body
Discuss each main idea in one or more paragraphs and support each main idea with facts, examples, and quotations.

Conclusion
Bring your report to a close by tying your ideas together. Summarize or restate your main idea(s) or draw conclusions.

Discuss and Decide

If you were writing about the aftermath of a hurricane on a community, what text structure would you use? Why?

Americans Are Eating Fewer Calories, So Why Are We Still **Obese?**

by Alexandra Sifferlin for *TIME*
Feb. 22, 2013

The good news: we're eating fewer calories. The bad news: that's not translating into lower obesity rates.

Two federal studies on the amount of calories Americans eat show that we are eating less than we did about a decade ago, and that we're also limiting the amount of fast food we consume.

Between 2007 to 2010, about 11.3% of daily calories came from from fast food, down from 12.8% reported between 2003 to 2006, according to data collected by the U.S. Center for Disease Control and Prevention (CDC). Fast food consumption decreased with age, with adults aged 60 and older eating the least of this type of food. For younger adults, non-Hispanic black adults reporting eating the most fast food, with more than one-fifth of their daily calories coming from fast food chains.

Not surprisingly, those who took in the most calories from fast food favorites also weighed the most. "The good news from this study is that as we get older, perhaps we do get wiser and eat less fast food," Samantha Heller, a clinical nutritionist at the NYU Center for Musculoskeletal Care in New York City told HealthDay. "However, a take-home message is that the study suggests that the more fast food you eat, the fatter you get."

The second study, also conducted by the CDC, looked at American kids aged 2 to 19 and found that boys were eating fewer calories, dropping from an average of 2,258 calories a day in 1999–2000 to approximately 2,100 calories in 2009–2010. The trend also applied to girls, who ate 76 fewer calories on average in the same time period. Most of this decline came in the form of carbohydrates; children continued to eat about the same amount of fats while increasing the protein they consumed.

"The children had a decrease in carbohydrates, and one of the carbohydrates is added sugars," says CDC researcher Cynthia L. Ogden, who oversaw the research. "There is evidence showing that added sugars have decreased in general, and that these things are related to obesity. I think it will be interesting to continue to watch these trends and see what happens nationally." Ogden says a major source of added sugar in diets comes from sugar-sweetened beverages, and

© Houghton Mifflin Harcourt Publishing Company

as research shows limiting this sweet drinks can curb weight gain, parents may be curbing the amount of sweetened sodas children drink.

But if Americans are eating less fast food overall, why are obesity rates still so high? As encouraging as the calorie data are, the decreases aren't significant enough to make a dent in upward trend of obesity. "To reverse the current prevalence of obesity, these numbers have to be a lot bigger," Marion Nestle, a professor of nutrition, food studies and public health at New York University told the *New York Times*. "But they are trending in the right direction, and that's good news."

It may depend on how you look at the data. According to Ogden, while obesity rates may be high, the latest statistics show they may be stable, and not continuing to climb upward. "The rate of obesity has been flat recently in both children and in adults and some studies have come out recently that have found a decrease in obesity or childhood obesity in some cities. Still, a third of U.S. adults are obese and 17% of children are obese, but given this relatively stability, I think that these two studies show very interesting results," says Ogden.

"I think [these findings] are a great start. I am happy to see there is a slight decrease. It still shows that for as much effort that has been put into messaging and positive nutrition promotion, we still have a lot of work to do. There are a lot of people who still need to be touched," says Laura Jeffers, a registered dietitian at Cleveland Clinic in Ohio.

Refining that message may require delving deeper in what Americans are eating, and addressing the balance between the amount of calories that we eat and the amount we burn off daily through physical activity. Jeffers speculates that even though fast food consumption is down, Americans may be eating unhealthy calories elsewhere. "I think that overall, people are not consuming the majority of their meals at fast food. Even-though maybe fast food has decreased, the majority of calorie consumption is not from the fast food restaurants. Looking at portion sizes and what people are getting in the home and the nutrition and health from those foods, should be another focus as to why the obesity rate is continuing to climb," she says.

And while eating less is a good way to start addressing the obesity epidemic, it may be that slimming the national waistline means we also have to boost the amount of exercise we get every day.

Discuss and Decide

According to this article, in what way does the message about obesity need to be "refined"?

Analyze a Student Model for Step 1

Hua chose to use a cause-and-effect structure for her essay. In it, Hua explains how excess sugar, salt, and fat in one's diet causes serious health risks. Ms. Steiner made her notes in red.

Hua's Model

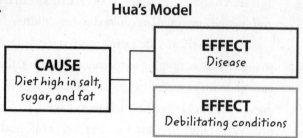

Hua Zhi
Ms. Steiner, English
February 7

Sugar, Salt, Fat: How to Deal with This Public Health **Triple Threat**

Adressing the reader directly is a great way to get his or her attention.

You are a careful and sensible person. You don't smoke, drink, or do illegal drugs. You wouldn't eat paint, or poison. So what's with the double cheeseburger, large fries, and soda for lunch? Chances are, you are not aware of the potentially devastating health effects of a diet too high in salt, sugar, and fat. And even if you know these foods are bad for you, you can't stop craving them. What's the source of this problem?

Biologically, our bodies are not as evolved as our environment. We are still pre-programmed to crave salt, sugar, and fat as these tastes were associated with scarce but important foods in prehistoric times. Back then we stayed healthy by ingesting as much salt, sugar and fat as we could find. Now that we have access to almost unlimited quantities of these once rare foods, our bodies have not yet dialed down the desire. We continue to crave and indulge to the point where it is not just unhealthy, it's actually killing us.

Diabetes, high blood pressure, heart attack, cancer, stroke...that is just the top of the list of diseases and debilitating conditions caused by a diet high in salt, sugar, and fat. This kind of diet leads to obesity—one of the leading causes of death worldwide. In the U.S., obesity-related diseases cost 147 billion dollars and lead to 300,000 premature deaths every year.

Yikes! That is an alarming number.

One possible approach to reduce the rates of obesity would be to regulate the food industry. After all, many other potentially unhealthy, addictive, or dangerous substances are carefully regulated—tobacco, alcohol, and prescription medicines, to name a few. The government could limit the amount salt or sugar allowed in a product, for example, or require meaningful health warnings on labels. Sugar, salt, and fat tap into the pleasure center of the brain, making them highly addictive. Companies take advantage of this scientific explanation for our cravings, and use marketing to make us unable to resist. Many health experts advise us to skip the fatty, sugary, or foods altogether. For example, it's impossible to eat just one or two cookies. You will want to keep going once you've started.

These changes seem feasible.

Is this a fact? Needs further explanation.

We're wired to want these tastes, but until the day that scientists create a craving-suppressor, exercising and eating healthy foods in moderation can aid in keeping the obesity epidemic from becoming any more problematic.

Close Read

Why do we crave unhealthy foods? Use evidence from the text in your response.

_____

_____

_____

_____

Terminology of Informative Essays

Read each term and explanation. Then look back at the essays you just read. Find an example from the essays to complete the chart.

Term	Explanation	Example from Essays
topic	The **topic** is a word or phrase that tells what the essay is about.	
text structure	The **text structure** is the organizational pattern of an essay.	
focus	The **focus** is the controlling, or overarching, idea that states the main point the writer chooses to make.	
supporting evidence	The **supporting evidence** is relevant quotations and concrete details that support the focus.	
domain-specific vocabulary	**Domain-specific vocabulary** is content-specific words that are not generally used in conversation.	
text features	**Text features** are design features that help organize the text, such as headings, boldface type, italic type, bulleted or numbered lists, sidebars, and graphic aids including charts, tables, timelines, illustrations, and photographs.	

Prose Constructed-Response

What elements were missing from Hua's essay? How would you revise her essay to make it more effective?

_____

_____

_____

1. Analyze   2. Practice   3. Perform

How can people prevent diseases from spreading?

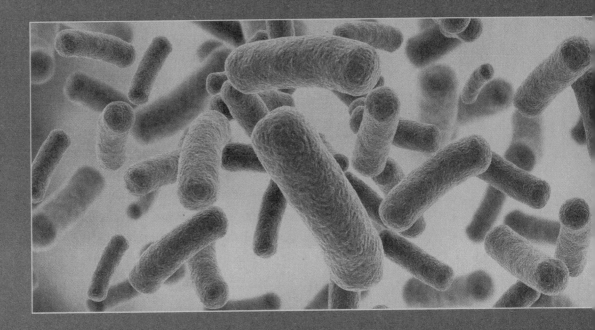

You will read:

▶ **A HISTORICAL ESSAY**
The Bubonic Plague

▶ **AN INFORMATIONAL ARTICLE**
Stopping the Spread of SARS

▶ **A BLOG**
On the Trail of Ebola

▶ **A PRESS RELEASE**
'Tis the Season for Flu Shots

You will write:

▶ **AN INFORMATIVE ESSAY**
How can people prevent diseases from spreading?

Source Materials for Step 2

AS YOU READ You will be writing an informative essay that synthesizes information from the following texts. Carefully study the sources in Step 2. Annotate by underlining and circling information that may be useful to you when you write your essay.

Source 1: Historical Essay

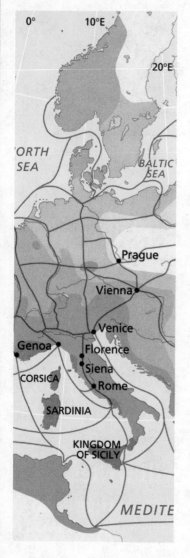

The Bubonic Plague

The people of fourteenth-century Europe were unprepared for what would become one of the greatest health crises in human history. Homes were made of mud, wood, and stone, and livestock crowded into the same rooms as their human caretakers. Indoor plumbing did not exist; personal hygiene might consist of an annual bath. Trash was dumped into yards, alleys, and roadways. Perhaps most important, science in the Middle Ages was anything but scientific, with doctors ascribing illnesses to bad air, witchcraft, and planetary fluctuations.

Around 1334, in Yunnan province of China, the bacterium *Yersinia pestis* began its long march westward. The bacterium commonly resides in the gut of fleas, which in turn feed on the blood of mammalian hosts such as marmots and rats. Rats were certainly the key vector animal in this epidemic. Hitching a ride on camel caravans along the Silk Road and then on trading ships in the Black, Mediterranean, and North Seas, *Y. pestis* made its way to Europe.

The disease was devastating. Infected people suffered severe fevers, vomited blood, and developed painfully swollen lymph glands, or buboes, that turned black and oozed pus. Most of the infected died within days. Historians argue about the exact death toll, but nobody disputes the scope of the catastrophe. Cities such as Paris, Florence, and Hamburg lost half their populations. Overall, Europe's population declined by a third or more, killing 20 million people.

Discuss and Decide

What made the spread of the bubonic plague especially hard to stop? Cite evidence in your response.

1. Analyze   2. Practice   3. Perform

Source 2: Informational Article

Stopping the Spread of SARS

by Namita Singh, MD, Ph.D.

In March 2003, the World Health Organization (WHO) issued an emergency travel advisory after it received reports of hundreds of suspected new cases of severe acute respiratory syndrome, or SARS, from around the globe.

"SARS," said Dr. Gro Harlem Brundtland, Director General of the World Health Organization, "is now a worldwide health threat."

Although scientists were still investigating the cause of the disease, its symptoms were known, and air travel was clearly helping spread the contagion across international borders. WHO therefore called on governments, airlines, and travelers to follow some common-sense protocols.

Any traveler with the following symptoms and history, stated WHO's advisory, should get immediate medical attention.

- High fever (greater than 100.4°F, or 38.0°C)
- Coughing, shortness of breath, difficulty breathing
- Close contact with someone diagnosed with SARS
- Recent travel to a country with reported cases of SARS

Scientists would later learn that SARS was caused by a virus in the same family as the virus that causes the common cold. Unsurprisingly, then, the disease could be transmitted through the air. When an infected person coughed or sneezed, tiny particles of SARS virus were expelled, which other people might breathe. If the particles landed on a surface—such as a hand, furniture, or clothing—the virus would die within hours. However, people who touched the surface before the virus died could become infected.

Discuss and Decide

Why was it important for people infected with SARS to avoid air travel?

Source 3: Blog

www.TrackingEbola.com

by Cassandra Adams, M.D. in partnership with Doctors International.

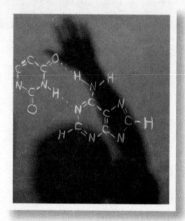

Enter your email address:

Subscribe me!

SEARCH

www.blogspot.com

www.TrackingEbola.com

On the Trail of Ebola

July 21

We arrive in Kampala at about 9 A.M. Most of the team has flown in from Europe, but a number of us have come all the way from New York. Everybody is exhausted, but there is little time for rest. A meeting with Ugandan government officials and World Health Organization experts has been scheduled for 11 A.M.

July 22

As we drive west from Kampala, bumping along rutted highways past verdant farms and remnant forests, my colleagues discuss what is known so far about this outbreak of Ebola. A "strange disease" was reported in the region a few weeks ago. Lab tests eventually identified the virus that causes Ebola Hemorrhagic Fever. So far, local health officials report that 20 people have contracted the disease. Fourteen of them have died.

July 23

After donning masks, gloves, and gowns, we descend on the local hospital like a group of alien invaders. Ebola patients have been quarantined in one wing of the hospital. They look scared. Through interpreters, we ask a lot of questions while trying to show as much compassion as possible. The virus is transmitted through bodily fluids, so a primary goal is to identify and isolate the infected. Healthcare workers are scouring the countryside for people with the telltale symptoms: backache, chills, diarrhea, fever, and vomiting.

July 24

We say goodbye to the hospital staff and doctors, who are doing heroic work. Last night, we learn, several patients began to bleed from their eyes and noses. There is no cure for Ebola fever.

Source 4: Press Release

Centers for Disease Control and Prevention

PRESS RELEASE | For Immediate Release　　　　　　October 28, 2013

'Tis the Season for Flu Shots

Washington, D.C.—The Centers for Disease Control (CDC) announced today that the flu season has begun. Flu, or influenza, is a contagious respiratory disease caused by any of a number of viruses. People should not underestimate the flu's severity. On average, 200,000 Americans contract the disease each year, and 36,000 will die. Young children, the elderly, and people with weakened immune systems are most likely to become seriously ill or die from the flu.

The CDC recommends that most people get a flu vaccine. There are different strains of flu, and scientists must identify which strains will be prevalent in the coming season before vaccine makers can begin preparing the millions of doses that will be required to keep the disease in check. Two kinds of vaccine are available: shots and nasal sprays. The nasal spray vaccine contains a live, weakened virus, and is recommended for healthy people between the ages of 2 and 49 who are not pregnant.

Other groups listed below should get the flu shot:
- People who care for children under the age of 6 months
- People who are 50 or older
- Healthcare workers
- Patients with chronic lung or heart disease
- Residents of nursing homes
- People with weakened immune systems
- Pregnant women

###

Discuss and Decide

Why are certain people supposed to receive killed instead of weakened flu viruses? Cite text evidence in your discussion.

Respond to Questions on Step 2 Sources

The following questions will help you think about the sources you've read. Use your notes and refer to the sources as you answer the questions. Your answers to will help you write your essay.

1 In what way is the Bubonic Plague different from the diseases mentioned in other texts?

   a. Doctors knew the cause of the plague.

   b. There was no cure for the plague.

   c. It was transmitted by animals.

   d. It was contained to one location.

2 Which words best support your answer to Question 1?

   a. "The bacterium commonly resides in the gut of fleas . . ." (Source 1)

   b. "There is no cure for Ebola fever." (Source 3)

   c. ". . . *Y. pestis* made its way to Europe." (Source 1)

   d. ". . . its symptoms were known, and air travel was clearly helping spread the contagion . . ." (Source 2)

3 Which of the following is *not* listed in the sources as a method of preventing diseases from spreading?

   a. washing hands

   b. wearing gloves around ill patients

   c. getting vaccinated

   d. boiling water before drinking it

4 Which of the following statements is true?

   a. Ebola is contracted through bodily fluids, coughing, and sneezing.

   b. The nasal spray vaccine for the flu is safe for pregnant women to use.

   c. Everyone who contracts Ebola dies.

   d. Ebola and the flu are treatable diseases.

5 Which statement best supports your answer to Question 4?

   a. "People should not underestimate the flu's severity." (Source 4)

   b. "Healthcare workers are scouring the countryside for people with the telltale symptoms . . ." (Source 3)

   c. "There are different strains of flu, and scientists must identify which strains will be prevalent in the coming season . . ." (Source 4)

   d. "There is no cure for Ebola fever." (Source 3)

6 **Prose Constructed-Response** What changes could those in fourteenth-century Europe have instituted to prevent the spread of the Black Plague? Cite evidence from the text in your response.

_____

_____

_____

_____

_____

_____

7 **Prose Constructed-Response** Make a claim about each source. Support your four claims with evidence from the text.

_____

_____

_____

_____

_____

_____

> Write an informative essay to answer the following
> question: How can people prevent diseases from
> spreading?

Planning and Prewriting

When you write informative text, you need to synthesize information from more than one
source.

 You may prefer to do your planning on the computer.

Analyze Sources

Look back over the sources you have read. Determine the strengths and limitations of each
source by considering whether it is appropriate for your audience and purpose. Complete
the chart to evaluate each source.

Source	Strengths and Limitations
Historical Essay The Bubonic Plague	
Informational Article Stopping the Spread of SARS	
Blog On the Trail of Ebola	
Press Release 'Tis the Season for Flu Shots	

   1. Analyze   2. Practice   3. Perform

Collect and Synthesize Information

Look back at your notes and look for opportunities to synthesize information—to make connections and combine facts in a way that provides a broader understanding of the subject. Complete the chart.

Topic	Evidence from Sources	Synthesis of Information
Causes of disease		
Spread of disease		
Treatment of disease		

Draft a Controlling Idea

Craft a controlling idea, or thesis statement. Your controlling idea should precisely identify what you want your audience to learn about how people can prevent the spread of infectious diseases.

Controlling Idea: _____

_____

_____

_____

Finalize Your Plan

Use your responses and notes from previous pages to create a detailed plan for your essay.

▶ Hook your audience with an interesting detail, question, or quotation.

▶ Clearly state the controlling idea.

▶ Organize the information in a logical way so that each new idea builds upon previous ideas.

▶ Use metaphors, similes, and analogies to help the reader understand complex ideas.

▶ Synthesize the ideas in the information you present.

▶ Restate your controlling idea and explain the significance of your topic

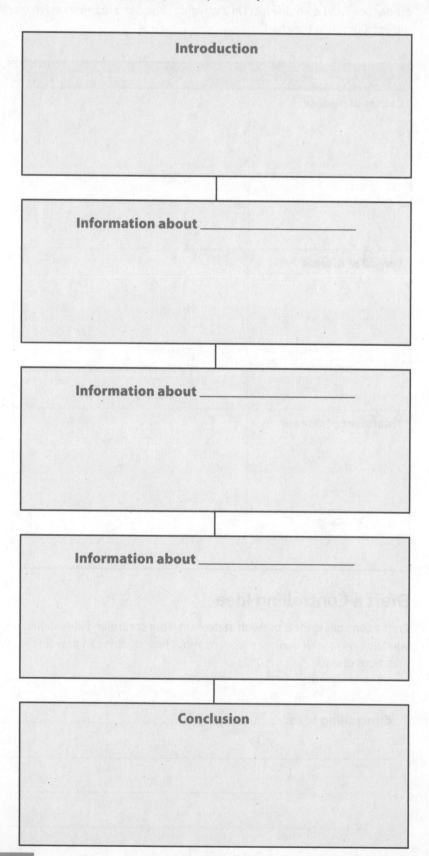

Introduction

Information about _____

Information about _____

Information about _____

Conclusion

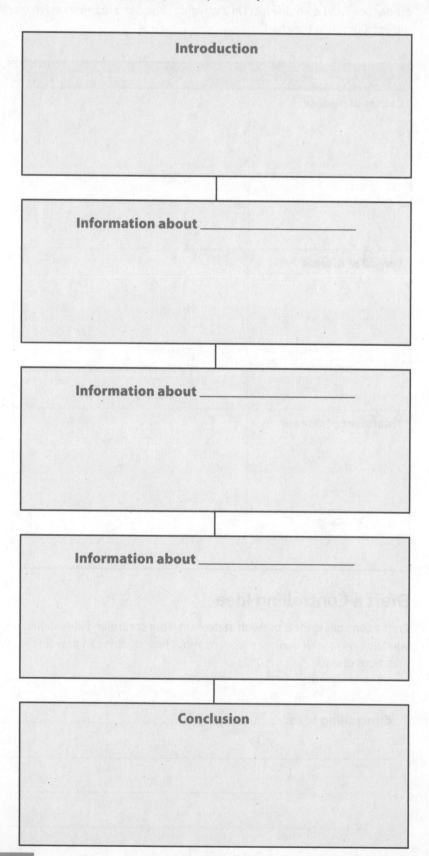

1. Analyze   2. Practice   3. Perform

Draft Your Essay

As you write, think about:

▶ **Audience:** Your teacher
▶ **Purpose:** Demonstrate your understanding of the specific requirements of an informative essay.
▶ **Style:** Use a formal and objective tone.
▶ **Transitions:** Use words and phrases such as *for example* or *because* to create cohesion, or flow.

Revise

Revision Checklist: Self Evaluation

Use the checklist below to guide your analysis.

 If you drafted your essay on the computer, you may wish to print it out so that you can more easily evaluate it.

Ask Yourself	Tips	Revision Strategies
1. Does the introduction present your controlling idea and grab the audience's attention?	Underline sentences in the introduction that engage readers.	Add an interesting question, fact, or observation to get the reader's attention.
2. Are your details relevant, do you present textual evidence for them, and do they support your controlling idea?	Circle textual evidence.	Add textual evidence if necessary.
3. Are appropriate and varied transitions used to clarify ideas?	Place a check mark next to each transitional word or phrase.	Add transitional words or phrases where needed to clarify the relationships between ideas.
4. Does the concluding section restate the controlling idea and explain the topic's signficiance? Does it give the audience something to think about?	Double underline the summary of key points in the concluding section. Underline the insight offered to readers.	Add an overarching view of key points or a final observation about the significance of the controlling idea.

Revision Checklist: Peer Review

Exchange your essay with a classmate, or read it aloud to your partner. As you read and comment on your classmate's essay, focus on logic, organization, and evidence—not on whether you agree with the author's controlling idea. Help each other identify parts of the draft that need strengthening, reworking, or a new approach.

What to Look for	Notes for My Partner
1. Does the introduction present the controlling idea and grab the audience's attention?	
2. Are your details relevant, do you present evidence for them, and do they support the controlling idea?	
3. Are appropriate and varied transitions used to clarify ideas?	
4. Does the concluding section restate the controlling idea and explain the topic's significance? Does it give the audience something to think about?	

Edit

 Edit your essay to correct spelling, grammar, and punctuation errors.

How can we improve our health?

You will read:

▶ **THREE INFORMATIONAL ARTICLES**

Wash Your Hands!

Quit Smoking

A Dozen Reasons to Exercise

You will write:

▶ **AN INFORMATIVE ESSAY**
How can we improve our health?

Part 1: Read Sources

Source 1: Informational Article

Wash Your Hands!
by Leonard Reiss, MD

AS YOU READ *Identify key terms that you might be able to use in your essay.*

NOTES

Handwashing is easy to do and it's one of the most effective ways to prevent the spread of many types of infection and illness in all settings—from your home and workplace to child care facilities and hospitals. Clean hands can stop germs from spreading from one person to another and throughout an entire community.

When should you wash your hands?

- Before, during, and after preparing food
- Before eating food
- Before and after caring for someone who is sick
10 - Before and after treating a cut or wound
- After using the toilet
- After changing diapers or cleaning up a child who has used the toilet
- After blowing your nose, coughing, or sneezing
- After touching an animal, animal feed, or animal waste
- After touching garbage

What is the right way to wash your hands?

- Wet your hands with clean running water (warm or cold) and apply soap.
- Rub your hands together to make a lather and scrub them well; be
20   sure to scrub the backs of your hands, between your fingers, and under your nails.
- Continue rubbing your hands for at least 20 seconds. Need a timer? Hum the "Happy Birthday" song from beginning to end twice.
- Rinse your hands well under running water.
- Dry your hands using a clean towel or air dry.

Washing hands with soap and water is the best way to reduce the number of germs on them. If soap and water are not available, use an alcohol-based hand sanitizer that contains at least 60% alcohol.

30 Alcohol-based hand sanitizers can quickly reduce the number of germs on hands in some situations, but sanitizers do not eliminate all types of germs.

Lather, Scrub, and Rinse

1. Lather hands with soap.

2. Rub both palms together.

3. Rub each finger and between fingers.

4. Rub palms with finger nails.

5. Rub back of hand with finger nails.

6. Wash thoroughly and towel dry.

Close Read

What is the the most effective way to clean your hands? Cite evidence from the text in your answer.

_____

_____

_____

_____

_____

_____

Quit Smoking

by Félice Danielle, MD

© Houghton Mifflin Harcourt Publishing Company • Image Credits: ©Anneka/Shutterstock

NOTES

Smoking harms nearly every organ of the body, causing many diseases and reducing the health of smokers in general. Quitting smoking has immediate as well as long-term benefits, reducing risks for diseases caused by smoking and improving health in general.

Smoking causes the following diseases and conditions:
- abdominal aortic aneurysm
- acute myeloid leukemia
- cancer of the bladder, cervix, esophagus, kidney, larynx, lung, mouth, pancreas, stomach, and throat
- 10 cataract
- coronary heart and cardiovascular diseases
- periodontitis
- pneumonia and chronic lung diseases
- reproductive effects and sudden infant death syndrome

Are you one of the more than 70 percent of smokers who want to quit? Then try following this advice.

1. **Don't smoke any cigarettes.** Each cigarette you smoke damages your lungs, your blood vessels, and cells throughout your body. Even occasional smoking is harmful.

20 2. **Write down why you want to quit.** Do you want to—

- Feel in control of your life?
- Have better health?
- Set a good example others?
- Protect your friends and family from breathing other people's smoke?

3. **Know that it will take commitment and effort to quit smoking.** Nearly all smokers have some feelings of nicotine withdrawal when they try to quit. Nicotine is addictive. Knowing this will help you deal with withdrawal symptoms that can occur, such as bad moods and really wanting to smoke.

30

There are many ways smokers quit, including using nicotine replacement products (gum and patches) or FDA-approved, non-nicotine cessation medications. But there is no easy way. For most people, the worst of the symptoms only last a few days to a couple weeks. Take quitting one day at a time, even one minute at a time—whatever you need to succeed.

4. **Get help if you want it.** Smokers can receive free resources and assistance to help them quit by calling 1-800-QUIT-NOW, or by visiting smokefree.gov (http://www.smokefree.gov), SmokefreeWomen (http://women.smokefree.gov), SfT (Smokefree Teen) (http://teen.smokefree.gov), or smokefree.gov (en Español) (http://espanol.smokefree.gov). Your doctor or dentist is also a good source of help and support.

40

Concerned about weight gain? It's a common concern, but not everyone gains weight when they stop smoking. Learn ways to help you control your weight as you quit smoking.

5. **Remember this good news!** More than half of all adult smokers have quit, and you can, too. Millions of people have learned to face life without a cigarette. Quitting smoking is the best step you can take to help stay healthy.

50

Discuss and Decide

What is the biggest benefit of quitting smoking? Cite text evidence in your response.

A Dozen Reasons to Exercise

by Rosie Alvarado-Martin, Certified personal trainer **and registered** dietitian

NOTES

1. Sleep A 16-week exercise program (30 to 40 minutes of brisk walking or low-impact aerobics four times a week) improved the quality, duration, and ease of falling asleep in healthy older adults. Exercise may improve sleep by relaxing muscles, reducing stress, or warming the body.

2. Gallstones Active women are 30 percent less likely to have gallstone surgery than sedentary women. In one study, women who spent more than 60 hours a week sitting at work or driving were twice as likely to have gallstone surgery as women who sat for less than 40 hours a week.

3. Colon Cancer The most active people have a lower risk of colon cancer—in two studies half the risk—compared to the least active people. Exercise may lower levels of prostaglandins that accelerate colon cell proliferation and raise levels of prostaglandins that increase intestinal motility. Increased motility may speed the movement of carcinogens[1] through the colon.

4. Diverticular Disease In one of the few studies that have been done, the most active men had a 37 percent lower risk of symptomatic diverticular disease than the least active men. Most of the protection against diverticular disease—pockets in the wall of the colon that can become inflamed—was due to vigorous activities like jogging and running, rather than moderate activities like walking.

5. Arthritis Regular moderate exercise, whether aerobic or strength-training, can reduce joint swelling and pain in people with arthritis.

---

[1] **carcinogens:** substances that cause cancer.

1. Analyze   2. Practice   3. Perform

6. **Anxiety and Depression** Getting people with anxiety or depression to do aerobic exercises like brisk walking or running curbs their symptoms, possibly by releasing natural opiates.

7. **Heart Disease** In one study, men with low fitness who became fit had a lower risk of heart disease than men who stayed unfit. In another, women who walked the equivalent of three or more hours per week at a brisk pace had a 35 percent lower risk of heart disease than women who walked infrequently. Exercise boosts the supply of oxygen to the heart muscle by expanding existing arteries and creating tiny new blood vessels. It may also prevent blood clots or promote their breakdown.

8. **Blood Pressure** If your blood pressure is already high or high-normal, low- or moderate-intensity aerobic exercise—three times a week—can lower it. If your blood pressure isn't high, regular exercise helps keep it that way.

9. **Diabetes** The more you move, the lower your risk of diabetes, especially if you're already at risk because of excess weight, high blood pressure, or parents with diabetes. In one study, women who walked at least three hours a week had about a 40 percent lower risk of diabetes than sedentary women.

10. **Falls and Fractures** Older women assigned to a home-based (strength- and balance-training) exercise program had fewer falls than women who didn't exercise. Exercise may prevent falls and broken bones by improving muscle strength, gait, balance, and reaction time.

11. **Enlarged Prostate (men only)** In one study, men who walked two to three hours a week had a 25 percent lower risk of benign prostatic hyperplasia (enlarged prostate) than men who seldom walked.

12. **Osteoporosis** Exercise, especially strength-training, can increase bone density in middle-aged and older people. Bonus: postmenopausal women who take estrogen gain more bone density if they exercise.

Discuss and Decide

Which benefits of exercise are more important for women? For men? Cite text evidence in your discussion.

Respond to Questions on Step 3 Sources

The following questions will help you think about the sources you've read. Use your notes and refer to the sources as you answer the questions. Your answers to will help you write your essay.

1 Which statement from "Wash Your Hands!" is best supported by the information in the image?

   a. "If soap and water are not available, use an alcohol-based hand sanitizer that contains at least 60% alcohol." (lines 27–28)

   b. "... be sure to scrub the backs of your hands, between your fingers, and under your nails." (lines 19–21)

   c. "After touching an animal, animal feed, or animal waste" (line 14)

   d. "Clean hands can stop germs from spreading from one person to another ..." (lines 4–5)

2 Which of these statements from "A Dozen Reasons to Exercise" provides the best scientific evidence for women to exercise more?

   a. "Regular moderate exercise, whether aerobic or strength-training, can reduce joint swelling and pain in people with arthritis." (lines 23–24)

   b. "The more you move, the lower your risk of diabetes, especially if you're already at risk because of excess weight, high blood pressure ..." (lines 40–42)

   c. "Exercise may lower levels of prostaglandins that accelerate colon cell proliferation and raise levels of prostaglandins that increase intestinal motility." (lines 13–15)

   d. "Older women assigned to a home-based (strength- and balance-training) exercise program had fewer falls than women who didn't exercise." (lines 45–47)

3 Which statement from "Quit Smoking" illustrates one challenge of quitting smoking?

   a. "There are many ways smokers quit, including using nicotine replacement products (gum and patches) ..." (lines 31–32)

   b. "Quitting smoking has immediate as well as long-term benefits, reducing risks for diseases caused by smoking and improving health in general." (lines 2–4)

   c. "Take quitting one day at a time, even one minute at a time—whatever you need to succeed." (lines 35–36)

   d. "It's a common concern, but not everyone gains weight when they stop smoking." (lines 44–45)

4 **Prose Constructed-Response** Which of the following offers the most health benefits: exercising, quitting smoking, or hand washing? Why? Cite evidence from the text in your response.

_____

_____

© Houghton Mifflin Harcourt Publishing Company

Part 2: Write

ASSIGNMENT

You have read a variety of texts on common health concerns. Now you will synthesize the information from these articles to answer this question: How can we improve our health? Include evidence from what you have read.

Plan

Use the graphic organizer to help you outline the structure of your informative essay.

Introduction

Information about _____

Information about _____

Information about _____

Conclusion

Draft

 Use your notes and completed graphic organizer to write a first draft of your essay.

Revise and Edit

 Look back over your essay and compare it to the Evaluation Criteria. Revise your essay and edit it to correct spelling, grammar, and punctuation errors.

Evaluation Criteria

Your teacher will be looking for:

1. *Statement of controlling idea*

▶ Is it clear what the controlling idea is?

▶ Did you support the controlling idea with details?

2. *Organization*

▶ Are the sections of your essay organized in a logical way?

▶ Is there a smooth flow from beginning to end?

▶ Is there a clear conclusion that supports the controlling idea?

▶ Did you stay on topic?

3. *Elaboration of evidence*

▶ Is the evidence relevant to the topic?

▶ Is there enough evidence?

4. *Language and vocabulary*

▶ Did you use a formal, noncombative tone?

▶ Did you use vocabulary familiar to your audience?

5. *Conventions*

▶ Did you follow the rules of grammar usage as well as punctuation, capitalization, and spelling?

Discoveries

UNIT 3
Literary Analysis

STEP 1

ANALYZE THE MODEL

Evaluate a student model about theme and figurative language in the poem "Missing the Sea."

STEP 2

PRACTICE THE TASK

Write a literary analysis essay that examines theme and the role of history in two poems called "Ozymandias."

STEP 3

PERFORM THE TASK

Analyze the themes of Shakespeare's "The Seven Ages of Man" and "Demeter," a Greek myth.

What matches the excitement of discovery? From the era of the great global exploration to the first steps on the moon, discovery is a pursuit that many find irresistible. How often have you arrived at a new place and asked yourself, "What lies beyond the horizon . . .?"

This unit presents two essays about the discovery of the tomb of Rameses II in the nineteenth century, which set Europe afire with the new science of Egyptology. It introduces you to Egyptian archaeology and ancient cultures that inspired noted nineteenth-century English poets Percy Bysshe Shelley and Horace Smith.

Discovery need not be exotic or strange. It may simply mean finding a new way of looking at something familiar, as poet Derek Walcott does in "Missing the Sea." By reading Shakespeare and the great myths of ancient Greece, we can discover emotions and experiences shared by all people and all times.

IN THIS UNIT, you will study a student's analysis of theme and figurative language in "Missing the Sea" by Derek Walcott. Then you will analyze two poems with the same title, "Ozymandias," and their use of historical background and theme. Finally, you will compare themes across genres in Shakespeare's "The Seven Ages of Man" and the myth of Demeter as retold by Edith Hamilton.

How can poetry help us rediscover the familiar?

You will read:

▶ **A BIOGRAPHY**
Derek Walcott: The Poet and His Craft

▶ **A POEM**
"Missing the Sea"

You will analyze:

▶ **A STUDENT MODEL**
Imagery and Figurative Language in Walcott's "Missing the Sea"

Source Materials for Step 1

Ms. Nam assigned her class a biography of Derek Walcott and his poem "Missing the Sea" to read and analyze. The notes in the side columns were written by Dylan, a student in Ms. Nam's class.

Derek Walcott:
The Poet and His Craft
by Lee Porter

He really was a child prodigy.

The recipient of the Nobel Prize in Literature, which was awarded to him in 1992, Derek Walcott was born in Castries, Saint Lucia, the West Indies, on January 23, 1930. He began writing at a young age, and his first published poem, "1944," appeared in the year of its title. A prodigy, he published two collections of poetry by the age of 19. He attended the University of the West Indies, and in 1951 published the volume *Poems*. Many other collections of poetry followed, most recently *White Egrets* (2010).

The subject of "Missing the Sea" is probably rooted in his Caribbean experiences.

Walcott strongly identifies with the fact that he is a Caribbean writer. Many of his poems address the status of the West Indies in the postcolonial period, and <u>his poetry delves deeply into the complexities of his Caribbean roots and identity</u>. Walcott has spoken of his role as a kind of pioneer, writing about West Indian people and places and describing them for the first time for the outside world. His work seeks to find a way to rebuild from the damage of colonialism—what he calls, in his own metaphor, that "shipwreck."

"Missing the Sea" also has three-line stanzas, but they don't rhyme.

Walcott's epic book-length poem *Omeros* was published in 1990 to international acclaim. The poem references Homer and characters from *The Iliad.* Composed in *terza rima,* or rhymed stanzas of three lines, the work resonates with Walcott's main themes: the beauty of the islands, Caribbean identity, and the role of the poet in describing and recreating the postcolonial world.

Walcott has achieved international fame.

The founder of the Trinidad Theater Workshop and the Boston Playwrights' Theatre at Boston University, Walcott is also a noted playwright, having published more than 20 plays. Walcott's honors include a MacArthur Foundation "genius" grant, a Royal Society of Literature Award, and the Queen's Medal for Poetry. He is an honorary member of the American Academy and Institute of Arts and Letters. He currently divides his time among Boston, St. Lucia, and New York City.

© Houghton Mifflin Harcourt Publishing Company

Missing the Sea

by Derek Walcott

Something removed (roars) in the ears of this house,
Hangs its drapes windless, (stuns) mirrors
Till reflections lack substance.

Some sound like the (gnashing) of windmills ground
To a (dead halt)
A deafening absence, (a blow.)

It hoops this valley, weighs this mountain,
Estranges gesture, pushes this pencil
Through a thick nothing now,

Freights cupboards with silence, folds sour laundry
Like the clothes of the dead left exactly
As the dead behaved by the beloved,

Incredulous, expecting occupancy.

How can something removed make a loud noise?

Strong words seem to emphasize the speaker's loss.

an oxymoron, like "something removed roars"

the strong "silence" again

Why do three-line stanzas now change to one line?

Discuss and Decide

Review Dylan's notes in the side column and summarize his response to the poem. Is it like yours, or is it different? Cite evidence from the notes and poem in your discussion.

Source Materials for Step 1

Read Dylan's literary analysis closely. The red side notes are the comments that his teacher, Ms. Nam wrote.

Dylan Shapiro
Ms. Nam, English
October 23

Imagery and Figurative Language in Walcott's "Missing the Sea"

Dylan, great job in interpreting the poem.

Born in 1930 on the island of Saint Lucia, and later living in Jamaica and Trinidad, the poet Derek Walcott reveals the influence of countless sailors in his poem "Missing the Sea." The speaker laments the terrible emptiness of a house when occupied by a person who loves the freedom of the sea. In "Missing the Sea," Walcott uses imagery of absence and loss to express the agony of a shore-bound sailor.

Your controlling idea shows me where you're going with your essay.

The speaker of the poem expresses his loss in images of sound or absence of sound of the wind. The wind is an effective synecdoche (using parts to represent the whole) because it represents attributes associated with the sea: water, salt, and vastness. Although absent from the house, this wind becomes "something removed [that] roars in the ears of the house." Strong verbs ("roars," "hangs," "stuns") describe a wind so strong it "weighs this mountain." Every image is harsh. Even those that emphasize the silence at the same time create a grating noise, "sound like the gnashing of windmills ground / To a dead halt." An oxymoron is also used to illustrate its power: "a deafening absence, a blow." It is this absent force that propels the sailor-poet to write his lament: "pushes this pencil." The present state of the housebound speaker is "thick nothing now," emphasizing the negative and empty conditions through alliteration.

Nice points about the language, especially the use of oxymoron.

This is very perceptive.

In the last full stanza, Walcott uses the images of objects found in the house (silent cupboards and "sour laundry"), again using synecdoche. The lack of sound is emphasized with the cupboard, and the negative sensory images continue with the laundry.

These domestic images grow even stronger through the simile of the clothes of the dead. The deceased person's clothes are left exactly as in life. So, too, the memory of the sea occupies the mind of the speaker, exactly as it did when he lived on the sea. He expects the sound of the wind but is left bereft and incredulous at its absence, just as one would feel looking at the clothes of a loved one who has passed away; the living, remaining person expresses his grief at the sight, just as the speaker of the poem expresses his loss. By comparing the absence of the wind to the death of a loved one, Walcott emphasizes the depth of his passion and longing for the sea.

Even if readers have not experienced a sailor's life, in "Missing the Sea," Walcott uses vivid imagery and strong figurative language to express the universal feeling of missing what you love most.

Good conclusion. Nice echo of your controlling idea and connection of the poem to your readers' own experiences.

Discuss and Decide

Reread the poem and literary analysis. What would you add to this interpretation of the poem? Cite evidence from both texts in your discussion.

Terminology of Literary Analysis

Read each word and explanation. Then look back at Dylan's literary analysis and find an example to complete the chart.

Term	Explanation	Example from Dylan's Essay
controlling idea	The **controlling idea** is an observation or assertion about the poem or piece of literature.	
theme	The **theme** is the underlying message about life or human nature that the writer wants the reader to understand.	
tone	The **tone** is the attitude the writer takes toward a subject.	
figurative language	**Figurative language** is language that communicates meanings beyond the literal meanings of words.	
imagery	The term **imagery** refers to words and phrases that create vivid sensory experiences for the reader.	
style	The **style** is the particular way in which a work of literature is written—not *what* is said but *how* it is said.	

What effects do past cultures have on literature?

You will read:

▶ **A BIOGRAPHY**
Rameses II ("Ozymandias")

▶ **HISTORICAL BACKGROUND**
The Ramesseum

▶ **TWO POEMS**
"Ozymandias"

"Ozymandias"

You will write:

▶ **A LITERARY ANALYSIS**
Analyze the treatment of theme and historical background in two poems entitled "Ozymandias"

Source Materials for Step 2

AS YOU READ You will be writing an essay analyzing two poems titled "Ozymandias." As you read, underline and circle information that may be useful to you when you write your essay.

Source 1: Biography

RAMESES II ("OZYMANDIAS")

by Philippa Crutchley

Rameses (or Ramesses) II, who reigned c1279 BC–1212 BC, was the third Egyptian pharaoh of the 19th dynasty. He is considered by many to be the greatest and most powerful pharaoh of the Egyptian empire. Although it cannot be supported by historical evidence, he is thought to be the great pharaoh who ruled during the Jewish exodus from Egypt in the story of Moses. Rameses is known for his military conquests, expanding the borders of the Egyptian empire in his time. He was a skilled general and led successful expeditions into Nubia in Africa and the areas of the Middle East known as the Levant and Canaan.

Rameses established the city of Pi Rameses in the Nile Delta as his capital and base of operations for a long campaign in Syria. In the early years of his rule, his armies invaded Syria and went to war against the Hittites, which ended in the bloody Battle of Kadesh. A few years after Kadesh, he again led Egypt in a war against the Hittites. After a decade of war, a peace treaty led to an era of peace and prosperity for the Egyptians and their Hittite enemies.

Rameses is perhaps best known for his vast architectural projects, including expansions and additions to cities, temples, and monuments. The ruins of these structures, discovered in the nineteenth century, sparked the new science of Egyptology and inspired the poems "Ozymandias" (Rameses's honorific in Greek) by Percy Bysshe Shelley and by Horace Smith. These poems mused upon how the vanities of this pharaoh, still proclaiming his greatness from the inscription on a broken, sand-eroded statue, had been laid low by the passage of time.

Egyptologists commonly believe that Rameses II lived into his nineties. He is thought to have taken the throne in his late teens and to have ruled for 67 years. His rule was severe, and he put down several insurrections among his own people. Thanks to the Egyptologists, he is noted for overseeing the construction of some of Egypt's most famous monuments and architecture, including many large statues of himself and the Ramesseum, a vast temple built solely to honor him.

1. Analyze   2. Practice   3. Perform

Source 2: Historical Background

The Ramesseum

by Anwar Hamdan

The Ramesseum was built by Rameses II as a funerary temple begun in the second year of his reign, and was erected on the west bank of the Nile River in Thebes in Upper Egypt. The temple is most famous for its 17-meter (57-foot) seated statue of Rameses II, of which only fragments remain. This huge, but shattered, colossus, which once proclaimed the power of the dead ruler, is the subject of both "Ozymandius" poems by Percy Bysshe Shelley and by Horace Smith. The walls of the Ramesseum, which is only half-preserved, are decorated with reliefs, including scenes depicting the Battle of Kadesh, Rameses's Syrian wars, and important religious festivals.

In 1798, fired by world conquest and the ideas of the Enlightenment, Napoleon Bonaparte invaded Egypt and took possession of its archaeological treasures, including the Ramesseum. The result was the vast 23-volume *Description of Egypt*, which introduced Egypt to Europe, and an in-depth study of the Ramesseum temple site. The French Egyptologists announced to an enthralled world that the temple was the "Tomb of Ozymandias" or "Palace of Memnon," of which Diodorus of Sicily, an ancient historian, had written in the first century BC.

In the early nineteenth century, Giovanni Belzoni, an engineer and a showman, was hired by the British to transport one of the two colossal granite heads depicting Rameses II to England. The seven-ton stone head arrived in London in 1818, where it was dubbed "The Younger Memnon." Reacting to the intense excitement about the statue's arrival and the tales of wonder about the desert treasures of the Ramesseum, Shelley wrote his famous sonnet, with Horace Smith following with his poem shortly thereafter.

One fallen colossus at the Ramesseum is particularly linked with Shelley's poem because of a cartouche (stamp with the Pharaoh's name) on it bearing Rameses's throne name, "User-maat-re Setep-en-re," the first part of which Diodorus transliterated into Greek as "Ozymandias." Shelley's "half sunk" and "shattered visage" lying on the sand is an accurate description of part of the demolished statue. The site remains a cautionary warning of the transitory nature of worldly fame and power.

Discuss and Decide

Summarize the important events of Rameses' rule. Then, explain the reaction of Europeans to the *Description of Egypt*. Cite evidence from both sources in your discussion.

Source 3: Poem

Ozymandias
by Percy Bysshe Shelley

I met a traveller from an antique land
Who said: Two vast and trunkless legs of stone
Stand in the desert. Near them, on the sand,
Half sunk, a shattered visage lies, whose frown,
5   And wrinkled lip, and sneer of cold command,
Tell that its sculptor well those passions read
Which yet survive, stamped on these lifeless things,
The hand that mocked them and the heart that fed;
And on the pedestal these words appear:
10   "My name is Ozymandias, king of kings:
Look on my works, ye Mighty, and despair!"
Nothing beside remains. Round the decay
Of that colossal wreck, boundless and bare
The lone and level sands stretch far away.

Discuss and Decide

What is ironic about the words on the pedestal? What should the mighty despair of, given the condition of the statue? Cite evidence from the poem in your discussion.

1. Analyze   2. Practice   3. Perform

Source 4: Poem

Ozymandias
by Horace Smith

In Egypt's sandy silence, all alone,
    Stands a gigantic Leg, which far off throws
    The only shadow that the Desert knows.
"I am great Ozymandias," saith the stone,
5   "The King of Kings; this mighty city shows
"The wonders of my hand." The city's gone!
    Nought but the leg remaining to disclose
The site of that forgotten Babylon.

We wonder, and some hunter may express
10 Wonder like ours, when through the wilderness
    Where London *stood*, holding the wolf in chase,
He meets some fragment huge, and stops to guess
    What wonderful, but unrecorded, race
    Once dwelt in that annihilated place.

Close Read

What comparison does the speaker make in this poem? According to the speaker, what do "we wonder"? Cite evidence from the poem in your response.

_____

_____

Respond to Questions on Step 2 Sources

These questions will help you analyze the texts you've read. Use your notes and refer to the sources to answer the questions. Your answers will help you write your essay.

1 Which of the following best expresses the theme of the two "Ozymandias" poems?

  a. Worldly power and glory are impermanent and fade with time.

  b. Two cultures encounter each other for the first time with tragic results.

  c. Rulers remain powerful and influential long after their deaths.

  d. No one lives forever.

2 Select the three pieces of evidence from the two "Ozymandias" poems that best support your answer to Question 1.

  a. "I met a traveller from an antique land" (Source 3, line 1)

  b. "And wrinkled lip, and sneer of cold command . . ." (Source 3, line 5)

  c. "'Look on my works, ye Mighty, and despair!'" (Source 3, line 11)

  d. ". . . Round the decay / Of that colossal wreck . . ." (Source 3, lines 12–13)

  e. "In Egypt's sandy silence, all alone . . ." (Source 4, line 1)

  f. "The only shadow that the Desert knows." (Source 4, line 3)

  g. ". . . The city's gone! / Nought but the leg remaining . . ." (Source 4, lines 6–7)

  h. "What wonderful . . . race / Once dwelt in that annihilated place." (Source 4, lines 13–14)

3 In what ways is the historical background pertinent to both poems?

  a. The poets involve themselves deeply in the new science of Egyptology.

  b. The poets provide a synopsis of the reign of Rameses II, describing his cruelty and warlike nature.

  c. The poets compare the history of Egypt to that of the British Empire.

  d. The poets both react to the wreckage of the real colossus of Rameses II, and muse on how time renders power and glory impermanent, if not irrelevant.

4 Select the three pieces of evidence from the two "Ozymandias" poems that best support your answer to Question 3.

  a. "I met a traveller from an antique land" (Source 3, line 1)

  b. ". . . that its scultptor well those passions read . . ." (Source 3, line 6)

  c. "Which yet survive, stamped on these lifeless things . . ." (Source 3, line 7)

  d. "Round the decay / Of that colossal wreck . . ." (Source 3, lines 12–13)

  e. "In Egypt's sandy silence, all alone" (Source 4, line 1)

  f. "The only shadow that the Desert knows." (Source 4, line 3)

  g. "'. . . this mighty city shows / 'The wonders of my hand.' The city's gone!" (Source 4, lines 5–6)

  h. "Nought but the leg remaining to disclose / The site of that forgotten Babylon." (Source 4, lines 7–8)

5 Prose Constructed-Response Compare the role of the speakers in the two poems. In what ways are they alike and different?

_____

_____

_____

_____

6 Prose Constructed-Response What were Rameses' passions or emotions? In what sense do those emotions survive? Cite evidence from the sources in your response.

_____

_____

_____

_____

7 Prose Constructed-Response Paraphrase the last stanza of Smith's "Ozymandias." What comparison does the speaker draw between Egypt and London? Cite evidence from the poem in your response.

_____

_____

_____

_____

Write a literary analysis that explores the question: In what ways are the two poems entitled "Ozymandias" similar, yet different in their treatment of historical background and theme?

Planning and Prewriting

When you compare, you tell how two things are similar. When you contrast, you tell how they are different.

 You may prefer to do your planning on the computer.

Decide on Key Points

Point		Shelley	Smith
1. Subject ☐ Alike　☑ Different		The great king still vainly proclaims his greatness.	The great king still vainly proclaims his greatness, but a hunter encountering a ruined London is introduced.
2. Theme ☐ Alike　☐ Different			
3. Genre ☐ Alike　☐ Different			
4. Use of historical hackground ☐ Alike　☐ Different			
5. Imagery ☐ Alike　☐ Different			
6. Speaker ☐ Alike　☐ Different			

Developing Your Topic

Before you write your essay, decide how you want to organize it. For both organizational strategies below, your essay will begin with an introductory paragraph and end with a concluding paragraph.

Point-by-Point Discuss the first point of comparison or contrast for both poems. Then move on to the second point. If you choose this organization, you will read across the rows of this chart.

Topic	Shelley's poem	Smith's poem	
1. Subject			
2. Theme			If you use this organizational structure, your essay will have a paragraph comparing or contrasting the subjects, followed by paragraphs comparing and contrasting the other points in your chart.
3. Genre			
4. Use of historical background			
5. Imagery			
6. Speaker			

Subject-by-Subject Discuss all the points about Shelley's poem before moving on to Smith's poem. If you choose this method, you will be reading across the rows of this chart.

Selection	Subject	Theme	Genre	Use of historical background	Imagery	Speaker
1. Shelley's poem						
2. Smith's poem						
If you use this organizational structure, your essay will have one or two paragraphs addressing all your points as they relate to Shelley's poem, followed by one or two paragraphs addressing all your points as they relate to Smith's poem.						

Finalize Your Plan

Use your responses and notes from previous pages to create a detailed plan for your essay. Fill in the chart below.

▶ Hook your audience with an interesting detail, question, or quotation.

▶ Identify what you will be comparing and contrasting, and state your controlling idea.

▶ Follow a framework like the one shown here to organize your main ideas and supporting evidence.

▶ Include relevant facts, concrete details, and other text evidence.

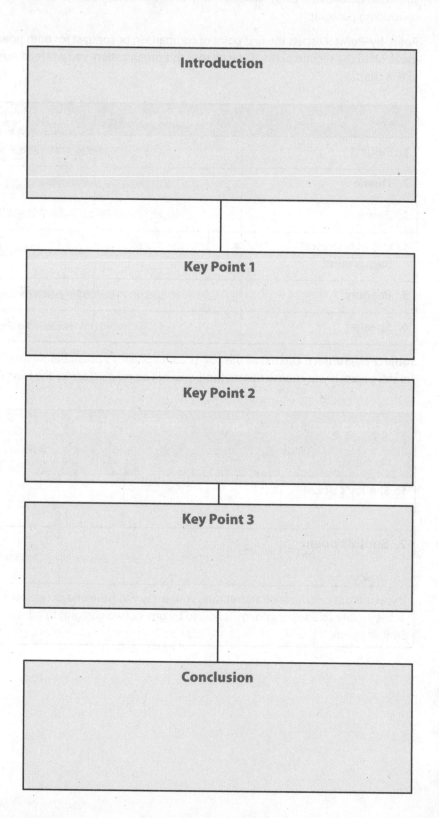

Introduction

Key Point 1

Key Point 2

Key Point 3

Conclusion

▶ Summarize the key points and restate your controlling idea.

▶ Include an insight that follows from and supports your controlling idea.

© Houghton Mifflin Harcourt Publishing Company

Draft Your Essay

As you write, think about:

▶ **Audience:** Your teacher

▶ **Purpose:** Demonstrate your understanding of the specific requirements of a literary analysis that compares theme and reference to historical background in two poems.

▶ **Style:** Use a formal and objective tone.

▶ **Transitions:** Use words and phrases such as *both, and, like,* and *in the same way* to show similarities, and words and phrases such as *but, yet, unlike, however, while, although, on the other hand,* and *by contrast* to show differences.

Revise

Revision Checklist: Self Evaluation

Use the checklist below to guide your analysis.

 If you drafted your essay on the computer, you may wish to print it out so that you can more easily evaluate it.

Ask Yourself	Tips	Revision Strategies
1. Does the introduction capture the readers' attention and include a controlling idea?	Draw a line under the compelling introductory text. Circle the controlling idea.	Add a compelling introductory sentence or idea. Make your controlling idea clear and precise.
2. Are there examples of ways in which themes of the poems are alike, and ways in which they are different? Are the comparisons and contrasts supported by evidence from the poems?	Underline each example. Circle the evidence from the texts and draw a line to the comparison or contrast it supports.	Add examples or revise existing ones to make them more valid. Provide evidence from the text.
3. Are appropriate and varied transitions used to compare and contrast, as well as to connect ideas?	Place a checkmark next to each transitional word or phrase. Add transitional words or phrases, where needed, to clarify the relationships between ideas.	Add words, phrases, or clauses to connect related ideas that lack transitions.
4. Is there a strong conclusion that follows from or is supported by the preceding paragraphs? Does it give the reader insight into the two works and their themes and use of historical background?	Put a plus sign next to the concluding statement. Star the text in the essay that supports or builds up to the conclusion. Underline the insight that is offered to readers.	Add an overarching view of key points or a final observation about the significance of the comparison and contrast.

Revision Checklist: Peer Review

Exchange your essay with a classmate, or read it aloud to your partner. As you read and comment on your classmate's essay, focus on how the comparisons and contrasts between the themes are supported by textual evidence. Help each other identify parts of the draft that need strengthening, reworking, or a new approach.

What To Look For	Notes for My Partner
1. Does the introduction grab the audience's attention and include a controlling idea?	
2. Are there examples of ways in which the themes and other aspects of the works are alike, and ways in which they are different? Are the comparisons and contrasts supported by evidence from the texts?	
3. Are appropriate and varied transitions used to connect, compare, and contrast ideas?	
4. Is there a strong conclusion that follows from or is supported by the preceding paragraphs? Does it give the reader something to think about?	

Edit

 Edit your essay to correct spelling, grammar, and punctuation errors.

How does literature help us answer our questions about life?

You will read:

▶ **A DRAMATIC MONOLOGUE**
"The Seven Ages of Man"

▶ **A MYTH**
"Demeter"

You will write:

▶ **A LITERARY ANALYSIS**
Analyze the universal themes of "The Seven Ages of Man" by William Shakespeare and the myth "Demeter" as retold by Edith Hamilton

Part 1: Read Sources

Source 1: Dramatic Monologue

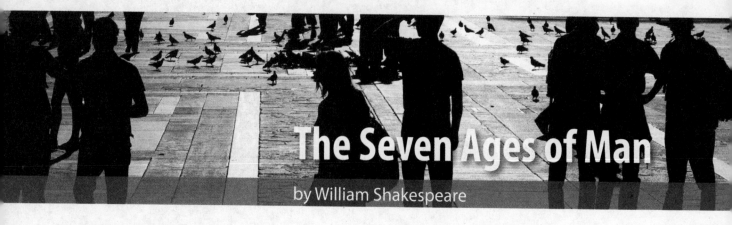

The Seven Ages of Man

by William Shakespeare

AS YOU READ *You will be writing a literary analysis that examines and intreprets universal themes across genres in "The Seven Ages of Man" by William Shakespeare and the myth" Demeter" retold by Edith Hamilton. As you read the dramatic monologue by the character Jacques (jā´ kwēz) from Shakespeare's play* As You Like It, *record comments or questions about the text in the side margins. Circle information that might be useful to you.*

NOTES

              All the world's a stage,
And all the men and women merely players;
They have their exits and their entrances,
And one man in his time plays many parts,
5 His acts being seven ages. At first the infant,
Mewling and puking in the nurse's arms;
And then the whining schoolboy, with his satchel
And shining morning face, creeping like snail
Unwillingly to school. And then the lover,
10 Sighing like furnace, with a woeful ballad
Made to his mistress' eyebrow. Then a soldier,
Full of strange oaths, and bearded like the pard,°
Jealous in honor, sudden and quick in quarrel,
Seeking the bubble reputation
15 Even in the cannon's mouth. And then the justice,
In fair round belly with good capon lined,
With eyes severe and beard of formal cut,
Full of wise saws and modern instances;
And so he plays his part. The sixth age shifts
20 Into the lean and slippered pantaloon,

---

12. pard: leopard

  1. Analyze   2. Practice   3. Perform

With spectacles on nose and pouch on side;
His youthful hose, well saved, a world too wide
For his shrunk shank; and his big manly voice,
Turning again toward childish treble, pipes
25 And whistles in his sound. Last scene of all,
That ends this strange eventful history,
Is second childishness and mere oblivion,
Sans° teeth, sans eyes, sans taste, sans everything.

---

28. sans: French for "without"

NOTES

Close Read

In the space below, list the seven stages of man that Jacques describes in his dramatic monologue.

_____

_____

_____

_____

Source 1: Myth

Demeter

retold by Edith Hamilton

AS YOU READ *Think about how this ancient myth explains nature's cycles. Record comments or questions in the side margins. Circle information that might be useful to you.*

NOTES

Demeter had an only daughter, Persephone (in Latin *Proserpine*), the maiden of the spring. She lost her and in her terrible grief she withheld her gifts from the earth, which turned into a frozen desert. The green and flowering land was icebound and lifeless because Persephone had disappeared.

The lord of the dark underworld, the king of the multitudinous dead, carried her off when, enticed by the wondrous bloom of the narcissus, she strayed too far from her companions. In his chariot drawn by coal-black steeds he rose up through a chasm in the earth, and
10 grasping the maiden by the wrist set her beside him. He bore her away, weeping, down to the underworld. The high hills echoed her cry and the depths of the sea, and her mother heard it. She sped like a bird over sea and land seeking her daughter. But no one would tell her the truth, "no man nor god, nor any sure messenger from the birds." Nine days Demeter wandered, and all that time she would not taste of ambrosia or put sweet nectar to her lips. At last she came to the Sun and he told her all the story: Persephone was down in the world beneath the earth, among the shadowy dead.

Then a still greater grief entered Demeter's heart. She left Olympus;
20 she dwelt on earth, but so disguised that none knew her, and, indeed, the gods are not easily discerned by mortal men. In her desolate wanderings she came to Eleusis° and sat by the wayside near a wall. She seemed an aged woman, such as in great houses care for the children or guard the storerooms. Four lovely maidens, sisters, coming to draw water from the well, saw her and asked her pityingly what she did there. She answered that she had fled from pirates who had meant to

---

22. Eleusis: ancient Greek city known for secret rituals performed by Demeter

1. Analyze   2. Practice   3. Perform

sell her as a slave, and that she knew no one in this strange land to go
to for help. They told her that any house in the town would welcome
her, but that they would like best to bring her to their own if she would
30 wait there while they went to ask their mother. The goddess bent her
head, in assent, and the girls, filling their shining pitchers with water,
hurried home. Their mother, Metaneira, bade them return at once and
invite the stranger to come, and speeding back they found the glorious
goddess still sitting there, deeply veiled and covered to her slender feet
by her dark robe. She followed them, and as she crossed the threshold to
the hall where the mother sat holding her young son, a divine radiance
filled the doorway and awe fell upon Metaneira.

She bade Demeter be seated and offered her honey-sweet wine,
but the goddess would not taste it. She asked instead for barley-water
40 flavored with mint, the cooling draught of the reaper at harvest time
and also the sacred cup given the worshipers at Eleusis. Thus refreshed
she took the child and held him to her fragrant bosom and his mother's
heart was glad. So Demeter nursed Demophoon, the son that Metaneira
had borne to wise Celeus. And the child grew like a young god, for daily
Demeter anointed him with ambrosia and at night she would place
him in the red heart of the fire. Her purpose was to give him immortal
youth.

Something, however, made the mother uneasy, so that one night
she kept watch and screamed in terror when she saw the child laid in
50 the fire. The goddess was angered; she seized the boy and cast him on
the ground. She had meant to set him free from old age and from death,
but that was not to be. Still, he had lain upon her knees and slept in her
arms and therefore he should have honor throughout his life.

Then she showed herself the goddess manifest. Beauty breathed
about her and a lovely fragrance; light shone from her so that the
great house was filled with brightness. She was Demeter, she told the
awestruck women. They must build her a great temple near the town
and so win back the favor of her heart.

Thus she left them, and Metaneira fell speechless to the earth and
60 all there trembled with fear. In the morning they told Celeus what had
happened and he called the people together and revealed to them the
command of the goddess. They worked willingly to build her a temple,
and when it was finished Demeter came to it and sat there—apart
from the gods in Olympus, alone, wasting away with longing for her
daughter.

© Houghton Mifflin Harcourt Publishing Company

That year was most dreadful and cruel for mankind over all the earth. Nothing grew; no seed sprang up; in vain the oxen drew the plowshare through the furrows. It seemed the whole race of men would die of famine. At last Zeus saw that he must take the matter in hand. He

70 sent the gods to Demeter, one after another, to try to turn her from her anger, but she listened to none of them. Never would she let the earth bear fruit until she had seen her daughter. Then Zeus realized that his brother must give way. He told Hermes to go down to the underworld and to bid the lord of it let his bride go back to Demeter.

Hermes found the two sitting side by side, Persephone shrinking away, reluctant because she longed for her mother.

At Hermes' words she sprang up joyfully, eager to go. Her husband knew that he must obey the word of Zeus and send her up to earth away from him; but he prayed her as she left him to have kind thoughts

80 of him and not be so sorrowful that she was the wife of one who was great among the immortals. And he made her eat a pomegranate seed, knowing in his heart that if she did so she must return to him.

He got ready his golden car and Hermes took the reins and drove the black horses straight to the temple where Demeter was. She ran out to meet her daughter as swiftly as a Maenad runs down the mountainside. Persephone sprang into her arms and was held fast there. All day they talked of what had happened to them both, and Demeter grieved when she heard of the pomegranate seed, fearing that she could not keep her daughter with her.

90 Then Zeus sent another messenger to her, a great personage, none other than his revered mother Rhea, the oldest of the gods. Swiftly she hastened down from the heights of Olympus to the barren, leafless earth, and standing at the door of the temple she spoke to Demeter.

Discuss and Decide

What is the result of Demeter's anger? Cite evidence from the text in your discussion.

"Come, my daughter, for Zeus, far-seeing, loud-thundering, bids you. Come once again to the halls of the gods where you shall have honor, where you will have your desire, your daughter, to comfort your sorrow as each year is accomplished and bitter winter is ended. For a third part only the kingdom of darkness shall hold her. For the rest you will keep her, you and the happy immortals. Peace now. Give men life
100 which comes alone from your giving."

Demeter did not refuse, poor comfort though it was that she must lose Persephone for four months every year and see her young loveliness go down to the world of the dead. But she was kind; the "Good Goddess," men always called her. She was sorry for the desolation she had brought about. She made the fields once more rich with abundant fruit and the whole world bright with flowers and green leaves. Also she went to the princes of Eleusis who had built her temple and she chose one, Triptolemus, to be her ambassador to men, instructing them how to sow the corn. She taught him and Celeus and the others her
110 sacred rites, "mysteries which no one may utter, for deep awe checks the tongue. Blessed is he who has seen them; his lot will be good in the world to come."

Close Read

How does Zeus resolve the conflict in this myth? Cite text evidence in your response.

_____

_____

_____

_____

Respond to Questions on Step 3 Sources

These questions will help you analyze the texts that you have read. Use your notes and refer to the sources in order to answer the questions. Your answers to these questions will help you write your essay.

1 **Prose Constructed-Response** How does the Demeter myth explain the cycles of the seasons?

_____

_____

_____

_____

_____

2 **Prose Constructed-Response** How are the themes of the monologue and the myth different?

_____

_____

_____

_____

_____

3 **Prose Constructed-Response** What about the themes of each text make it universal? In what ways are the two themes alike?

_____

_____

_____

_____

_____

Part 2: Write

ASSIGNMENT

Write a literary analysis that compares and interprets the universal themes in "The Seven Ages of Man" by Shakespeare and "Demeter" as retold by Edith Hamilton.

Plan

Use the graphic organizer to help you outline the structure of your literary analysis.

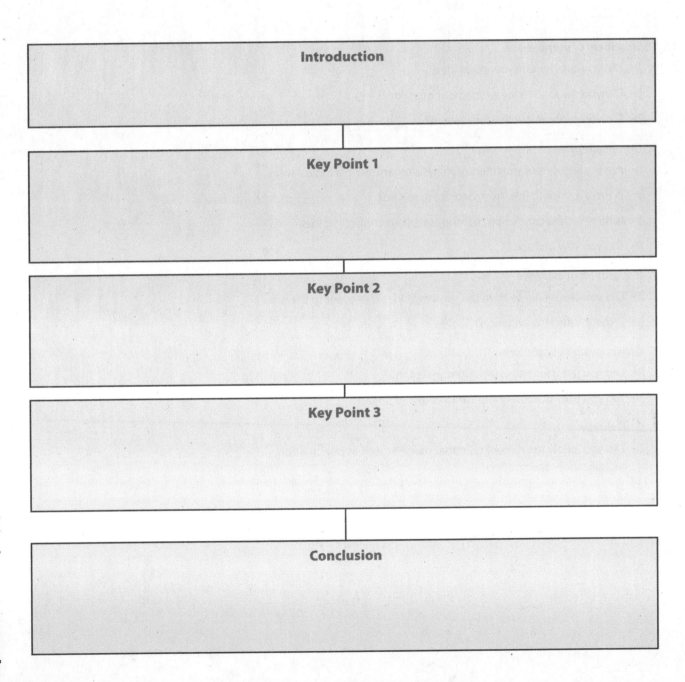

Introduction

Key Point 1

Key Point 2

Key Point 3

Conclusion

Draft

 Use your notes and completed graphic organizer to write a first draft of your literary analysis.

Revise and Edit

 Look back over your essay and compare it to the Evaluation Criteria. Revise your literary analysis and edit it to correct spelling, grammar, and punctuation errors.

Evaluation Criteria

Your teacher will be looking for:

1. *Statement of purpose*

    ▶ Did you clearly state your main idea?

    ▶ Did you respond to the assignment question?

    ▶ Did you support it with valid reasons?

2. *Organization*

    ▶ Are the sections of your literary analysis organized in a logical way?

    ▶ Is there a smooth flow from beginning to end?

    ▶ Is there a clear conclusion that supports your controlling idea?

    ▶ Did you stay on topic?

3. *Elaboration of evidence*

    ▶ Did you cite evidence from the sources, and is it relevant to the topic?

    ▶ Is there sufficient evidence?

4. *Language and vocabulary*

    ▶ Did you use a formal, essay-appropriate tone?

    ▶ Did you use vocabulary familiar to your audience?

5. *Conventions*

    ▶ Did you follow the rules of grammar usage as well as punctuation, capitalization, and spelling?

On Your Own

RESEARCH SIMULATION

Argumentative Essay

In civics class, your teacher has assigned an argumentative essay on the criminal justice system. You have chosen the topic of solitary confinement in prisons.

First you will review three articles about solitary confinement. After you have reviewed these sources, you will answer some questions about them. You should first skim the sources and the questions and then go back and read them carefully.

In Part 2, you will write an argumentative essay about whether you agree or disagree that solitary confinement should be abolished in U.S. prisons.

Time Management: Argumentative Task

There are two parts to most formal writing tests. Both parts of the tests are timed, so it's important to use your limited time wisely.

Part 1: Read Sources and Answer Questions

Preview the Assignment

35 minutes

You will have 35 minutes to read several articles about solitary confinement in U.S. prisons. You will also answer questions about the three sources.

35 minutes! That's not much time.

Preview the questions so you'll know which information you'll need to find as you read.

How Many?

How many pages of reading?

→ How many multiple-choice questions?

→ How many prose constructed-response questions?

How do you plan to use the 35 minutes?

Underline, circle, and take notes as you read. You probably won't have time to reread.

Estimated time to read:

This is a lot to do in a short time.

Source #1: "The Cost of Solitary Confinement"		minutes
Source #2: "Could This Be the End of . . . ?"		minutes
Source #3: "Controversial Study Supports Use of Solitary"		minutes
Estimated time to answer questions?		minutes
Total	**35**	**minutes**

Any concerns?

_____

_____

_____

_____

Part 2: Write the Essay

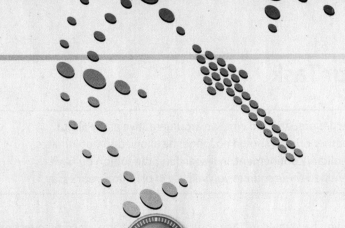

How much time do you have? Pay attention to the clock.

Plan and Write an Argumentative Essay

85 minutes

You will have 85 minutes to plan, write, revise, and edit your essay.

Your Plan

Before you start to write, decide on your precise claim and reasons. Then think about the evidence you will use to support your reasons.

How do you plan to use the 85 minutes?

Estimated time for planning the essay?	minutes
Estimated time for writing?	minutes
Estimated time for editing?	minutes
Estimated time for checking spelling, grammar, and punctuation?	minutes
Total	**85 minutes**

Be sure to leave enough time for this step!

Notes:

_____

_____

_____

_____

_____

Reread your essay, making sure that the points are clear. Check that there are no spelling or punctuation mistakes.

▶ Your Task

You are preparing to write an argumentative essay about whether prisons should no longer be allowed to put inmates in solitary confinement. In researching the topic, you have identified three sources you will use in planning your essay.

After you have reviewed the sources, you must answer some questions about them. Briefly skim the sources and the questions that follow. Then, go back and read the sources carefully so you will have the information you will need to answer the questions. Take notes on the sources as you read. You may refer back to your notes at any time during Part 1 or Part 2 of the performance task.

▶ Part 1 (35 minutes)

You will now read the sources. After carefully reading the sources, use the rest of the time in Part 1 to answer the four questions about them. Though your answers to these questions will help you think about what you have read and plan your essay, they will also be scored as part of the test.

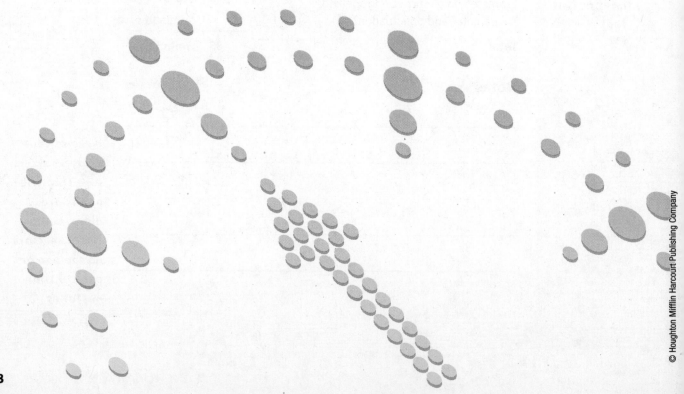

The Cost of
Solitary Confinement

The New York Times, Editorial   *December 13, 2012*

The New York Legislature greatly improved the treatment of mentally ill inmates in 2008, when it required the prison system to place seriously mentally ill inmates who violate rules into a treatment program instead of solitary confinement, where they were more likely to harm themselves.

A lawsuit filed last week [2012] by The New York Civil Liberties Union, however, suggests that the system is still misusing punitive isolation, not just for some of the mentally ill, but for a broad range of the system's 55,000 inmates.

10 Most prison systems use isolation selectively, singling out violent people who present a danger to guards and other inmates. The lawsuit asserts that New York uses isolation as routine punishment for minor, nonviolent offenses—more than any other system in the country.

The plaintiff in the suit, Leroy Peoples, is a 30-year-old with a history of mental illness who was twice sentenced to solitary confinement. In 2005, he was sentenced to six months for "unauthorized possession of nutritional supplements" that were available for sale in the prison commissary. In 2009, he was sentenced to three years in isolation for having unauthorized legal materials.

20 According to court documents, between 2007 and 2011, the state imposed 70,000 isolation sentences for offenses like having an "untidy cell or person," or for "littering," "unfastened long hair" or an "unreported illness." On any given day, about 4,300 of the system's inmates are locked down for 23 hours a day in tiny concrete cells, many of them destined to remain there for years. As additional punishment, prison officials can deny food, exercise, bedding or showers.

The suit charges that New York's system is arbitrary and, therefore, unconstitutional. It also suggests that African-American inmates are more often banished to isolation, and for longer periods of time, than 30 inmates from other racial groups. However the court decides this case, it seems clear that New York's isolation policy is inhumane and counterproductive, requiring clearer guidelines from the Legislature as to when isolation can and cannot be used.

Am I on Track?

Actual Time Spent Reading

SOURCE #2:

Could This Be the End of Solitary Confinement in Prisons?

by Su-chin Lee

NOTES

The question is a divisive one: should prisons continue to use solitary confinement? Solitary is often used as a form of punishment for violent infractions, such as attacking a correctional officer. However, solitary confinement is not always used judiciously, prompting proponents of alternative methods to argue that the time for solitary confinement has ended, and the time for rehabilitation has arrived.

The practice of isolating inmates involves their relocation to a roughly twelve-by-eight-foot cell, usually without windows. For twenty-three hours, a prisoner remains alone in the cell, and is removed for one hour in that period to exercise or shower.

Those who protest solitary confinement contend that the practice does more harm than good. A number of prisoners who are placed in isolation have mental illnesses before they enter, and their illnesses are only exacerbated by their time in a small cell. The psychological damage done to the prisoners placed in solitary confinement can be long term. Inmates who have been in solitary for years can have trouble reintegrating into the prison population—many of those who have been in isolation end up returning to solitary. Adjusting to the world outside of the prison is made that much more difficult, especially with inmates who may have become more violent during their time in isolation.

Solitary confinement is also argued to be too costly. The construction of solitary cells alone is more than the average cost of a prison that holds a general inmate population. Solitary cells can cost as much as three times the expense of a normal prison cell. When prisons turn to solitary confinement as more the rule than the exception, the costs grow.

Prisons across the U.S. are considering rehabilitative program in place of solitary confinement. Some of these programs would include "self-repair" and "moral recognition" therapy. These programs are aimed at an individual's potential to reform. For example, rather than being placed in an isolated environment, inmates would undergo classes such as anger management courses. Programs that address drug abuse, or teach a trade, could help transform troubled prisoners into productive members of society. These initiatives would save money for the duration of the prisoner's stay in the system, but they would also help prevent violence upon the prisoner's release into the general prison population and the world beyond.

Sending out reformed inmates who have been through rehabilitative programs is the best way to ensure that the problem does not continue to replicate itself. If something good can come out of incarceration, it seems foolhardy to let that opportunity go to waste. The experiment of solitary confinement has failed, so exploring other avenues seems a worthwhile endeavor.

NOTES

Am I on Track?

Actual Time Spent Reading

The Congressional Quarterly Researcher *is a publication of the U. S. Congress, reporting on research for the benefit of senators and representatives.*

Controversial Study Supports Use of Solitary

Inmates claim no ill effects, but critics cite flaws in research.

by Peter Katel

NOTES

Until recently, supporters of long-term solitary confinement had little academic research to back up what their experience told them: that placing inmates in isolation for long periods—is an indispensable tool in running a prison system.

Now, a controversial study based on research among Colorado prisoners is filling the gap—at least as far as advocates of solitary confinement are concerned.

The results, published in 2010 by the Justice Department's National Institute of Justice, are based on psychological tests administered to about 250 Colorado prisoners—some mentally ill—in both solitary and in the prison system's general population. The average length of a stay in solitary in Colorado is two years, but the study doesn't say how long each study participant in solitary had spent there. The tests included prisoners' self-assessments of their own psychological condition.

A report on the study, co-written by Maureen L. O'Keefe, research director for the Colorado Department of Corrections, concluded that "there was initial improvement in psychological well-being across all study groups." What's more, it said "elevations in psychological and cognitive functioning that were evident at the start of the study remained present at the end of the study."

The report noted that researchers had not expected these results and that the study's conclusions contradicted "the bulk of literature" indicating that solitary confinement "is extremely detrimental to inmates with and without mental illness."

"People who rail against isolated confinement were very disappointed in the outcome of the report," says Eugene Atherton, a Pueblo, Colo.-based prison management consultant and former Colorado warden. "The research showed the opposite of what they had hoped would be proved."

30   Advocates of solitary confinement have used the study to support their view that isolating prisoners for long periods—usually known in the field as "administrative segregation" or "ad seg"—is a legitimate form of punishment and necessary for maintaining control of inmate populations.

Last June, Charles E. Samuels Jr., director of the Federal Bureau of Prisons, told the Senate Judiciary Committee's Constitution, Civil Rights and Human Rights Subcommittee that the study found that "no negative effect on individuals in restrictive housing has occurred."

But opponents of solitary confinement argue that the study is flawed and should not be used to shape prison policy.

40   O'Keefe and study adviser Jeffrey L. Metzner, a University of Colorado psychiatry professor and longtime expert on mental health in prison, acknowledged that the report shouldn't be taken as conclusive evidence that applies to all long-term solitary nationwide. "This study may not generalize to other prison systems, especially those that have conditions of confinement more restrictive and/or harsher than CSP [Colorado State Penitentiary]," they wrote.

Despite the caveats, the report has generated a furious response from corrections experts, who have concluded that isolation damages prisoners who were either mentally ill to start with or mentally healthy when their 50 isolation began.

Stuart Grassian and Terry Kupers, psychiatrists with long professional track records in correctional mental health, argued, for example, that relying on prisoners to assess their own psychological conditions constitutes a fundamental flaw of the study. The testing materials the researchers used weren't designed specifically for prison inmates, Grassian and Kupers wrote. Prisoners in the study sample were told that the purpose was to research adjustment to prison life.

"Anyone with a background in corrections knows that is not the kind of information an inmate would likely expose," Grassian and Kupers 60   wrote. "It could harm him, even surreptitiously, for example at a parole hearing or in hearings to determine whether he could progress to higher levels in [administrative segregation]."

The study's critics may have feared that it would be used to justify maintaining or even expanding the number of prisoners in solitary confinement. But that has not been the result, at least in Colorado.

Am I on Track?

Actual Time Spent Reading

Part 1 Questions

Answer the following questions. You may refer to your reading notes, and you should cite text evidence in your responses. Your answers to these questions will be scored. You will be able to refer to your answers as you write your essay in Part 2.

1 What is a key counterclaim made by critics of the research study discussed in Source #3?

   a. Many of the prisoners who filled out the research questionnaires were mentally ill.

   b. The researchers who conducted the study showed bias in their dealings with prisoners.

   c. The researchers who conducted the study used an unreliable sample in their data collection.

   d. Some of the prisoners who filled out the research questionnaires may not have answered truthfully.

2 **Prose Constructed-Response** On what grounds did the Civil Liberties Union bring the lawsuit against New York's use of solitary confinement? Support your response with evidence from Source #1.

_____

_____

_____

3 **Prose Constructed-Response** Explain the alternatives to traditional solitary confinement that are being considered at some prisons. Support your response with evidence from Source #2.

_____

_____

_____

4 **Prose Constructed-Response** Briefly summarize the results of the study in Source #3 that supports the use of solitary confinement. Use your own words unless you are citing information from the source, and make sure your summary is free from bias or opinion.

_____

_____

_____

_____

▶ Part 2 (85 minutes)

You will have 85 minutes to review your notes and sources and to plan, draft, edit, and revise your essay. While you may use your notes and refer to the sources, your essay must represent your original work. You may refer to your responses to Part 1 questions, but you cannot change those answers. Now read your assignment and the information about how your writing will be scored; then begin your work.

Your Assignment

The deadline for your civics assignment is approaching, so you need to start writing your argumentative essay. Remember, your essay should explain whether you agree or disagree that solitary confinement should be abolished in U.S. prisons. When writing your essay, find ways to use information from the three sources to support your argument. A good argumentative essay should include a strong claim, and it should address opposing arguments.

Argumentative Essay Scoring

Your essay will be scored using the following:

1. **Organization/purpose:** How well did you express your claim, address opposing claims, and support your claim with logical ideas? How well did your ideas flow from beginning to end? How effective was your introduction and conclusion?

2. **Evidence/elaboration:** How well did you incorporate relevant information from the sources? Did you use specific titles or numbers in referring to the sources? How strong is the elaboration for your ideas? Did you clearly state your ideas in your own words in a way that is appropriate for your audience and purpose?

3. **Conventions:** How well did you follow the rules of grammar, punctuation, capitalization, and spelling?

Now begin work on your essay. Manage your time carefully so that you can:

- plan your essay, using your notes

- write your essay

- revise and edit your final draft

TASK 2

RESEARCH SIMULATION

Informative Essay

A local STEM (science, technology, engineering, and mathematics) program is sponsoring an essay contest on the history of mathematics. You have decided to write an essay on number systems for the contest.

First you will review two articles about number systems. After you have reviewed these sources, you will answer some questions about them. You should first skim the sources and the questions and then go back and read them carefully.

In Part 2, you will write an informative essay about how number systems have changed over time.

Time Management: Informative Task

There are two parts to most formal writing tests. Both parts of the tests are timed, so it's important to use your time wisely.

Part 1: Read Sources and Answer Questions

Preview the Assignment

35 minutes

You will have 35 minutes to read three selections about number systems. You will also answer questions about the sources.

35 minutes! That's not much time.

How Many?

Preview the questions so you'll know which information you'll need to find as you read.

How many pages of reading?

→ How many multiple-choice questions?

→ How many prose constructed-response questions?

How do you plan to use the 35 minutes?

Underline, circle, and take notes as you read. You probably won't have time to reread.

This is a lot to do in a short time.

Estimated time to read:

    Source #1: "Abacists and Algorists" — minutes

    Source #2: "The Modern Place-Value System" — minutes

Estimated time to answer questions? — minutes

Total — **35 minutes**

Any concerns?

_____

_____

_____

_____

_____

Part 2: Write the Essay

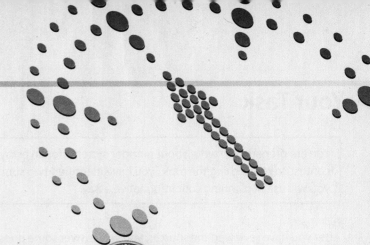

How much time do you have? Pay attention to the clock!

Plan and Write an Informative Essay

85 minutes

You will have 85 minutes to plan, write, revise, and edit your essay.

Your Plan

Before you start writing, decide how you will organize your informative essay.

How do you plan to use the 85 minutes?

Be sure to leave enough time for this step!

Estimated time for planning the essay?		minutes
Estimated time for writing?		minutes
Estimated time for editing?		minutes
Estimated time for checking spelling, grammar, and punctuation?		minutes
Total	**85**	**minutes**

Notes:

_____

_____

_____

_____

_____

_____

Reread your essay, making sure that the points are clear. Check that there are no spelling or punctuation mistakes.

▶ Your Task

You are preparing to write about number systems for an essay contest. In researching the topic, you have identified two sources you will use in planning your informative essay.

After you have reviewed the sources, you will answer some questions about them. Briefly skim the sources and the questions that follow. Then, go back and read the sources carefully so you will have the information you will need to answer the questions. Take notes on the sources as you read. You may refer back to your notes at any time during Part 1 or Part 2 of the performance task.

▶ Part 1 (35 minutes)

You will now read the sources. After carefully reading the sources, use the rest of the time in Part 1 to answer the three questions about them. Though your answers to these questions will help you think about what you have read and plan your essay, they will also be scored as part of the test.

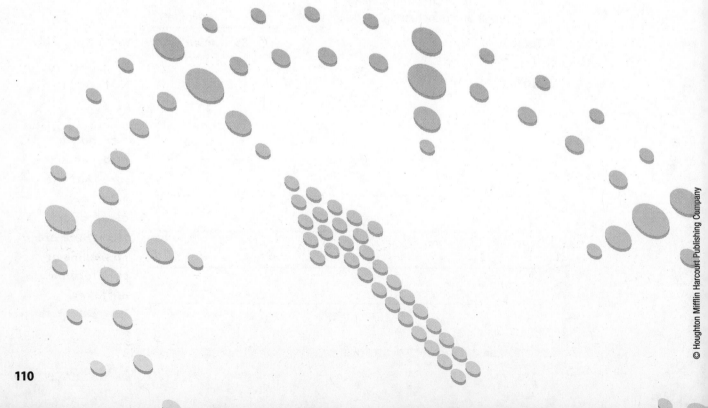

Abacists and Algorists

by Steve McGrath

NOTES

You may be familiar with Roman numerals, those numbers from ancient times that mostly show up on clock faces and in the numbering of Super Bowls. There was a time in Europe when Roman numerals were used to represent all counting numbers. But even in those times, Roman numerals were not used for calculations because adding, subtracting, multiplying, and dividing with the numerals was impractical. Instead, most people used something called an abacus to do arithmetic, which was a hand-held counting device consisting of a frame and parallel rods with moveable counters.

10   When the modern decimal system was first introduced in Europe, it offered an efficient way to compute all the arithmetic operations without the need for an abacus. Surprisingly, the decimal system was not immediately accepted. A bitter dispute arose between two opposing factions, the "algorists" and the "abacists." Those who favored the new Hindu-Arabic decimal system were called algorists, a word which stems from *Algoritmi*, the Latin translation of al-Khwarizmi, the name of an accomplished Persian mathematician. The abacists were those who favored the continued use of the abacus to do arithmetic. What followed was centuries of disagreement before the modern number system was

20   adopted throughout Europe in about AD 1500.

One of the factors that delayed acceptance of the decimal system was the fact that computation with an abacus was widespread and familiar. Also, the advantages of the new system were not apparent at first, because calculations were done in sand or by using some other erasable substance. After each calculation, the problem was erased before another calculation was done. It was not until paper was more available centuries later that the value of having records of calculations was a tipping factor in the debate.

The Roman Catholic church also played a role in the debate. The

30   church viewed the Hindu-Arabic numerals with suspicion, so church officials supported the use of the traditional Roman numerals.

The different interests of mathematicians and merchants played a role in the debate as well. Mathematicians were more invested in using numbers to record measurements, for which Roman numerals worked well. Merchants needed to perform more calculations, some of them very complex. At some point, merchants became enthusiastic about the new methods of calculation.

Italy played a significant role in the acceptance of the place-value system.[1] As Italy was a trade power in the world, Italian merchants
40 traded with Arabs and commonly used place values in their transactions. Italians taught place values as a way of computing. In fact, Leonardo of Pisa, a famous Italian mathematician, argued strongly for the use of the new decimal system in his book *Liber Abaci*.

Technology may have played the final role in the debate. When the printing press was invented in the 15th century, Arabic numerals became standardized with the result that there was a standard way of representing numbers and calculations.

---

[1] **place-value system:** a number system where the position of a digit within a number determines its value.

Am I on Track?

Actual Time Spent Reading

SOURCE #2:
The Modern Place-Value System

by Dayo Jackson

The number system that we use today—with ten digits and numbers represented with place values—is a system that we largely take for granted. Yet, because of the efficiency of the number system, it is a language that is shared across the entire world.

The system is called the Hindu-Arabic system to reflect the role of Indian and Muslim mathematicians in its development. Prior to the invention of the modern system, many number systems were in use around the world. In Europe, Roman numerals were still in use.

To see the usefulness of Arabic numerals, compare what is needed
10 to represent numbers such as 49 or 88 with Arabic numerals with the representation of the same numbers with Roman numerals.

Arabic and Roman Numerals		
1 = I	2 = II	4 = IV
5 = V	10 = X	50 = L
49 = XLIX		88 = LXXXVIII

Computing with Roman numerals is even more difficult. Some of the symbols indicate subtraction. For example, the representation of 4 as IV means to subtract 1 from 5. The result is that addition of two numbers cannot be done by adding on the values of the individual symbols. For example,

$$\begin{array}{r} XLIX \\ + LXXXVIII \\ \hline \end{array} \qquad \begin{array}{r} 49 \\ + 88 \\ \hline \end{array}$$

To add 49 + 88 using Roman numerals, it would not be helpful to add 10 for each of the X's that appear. This is because the first X in 49 means to subtract 10, whereas the other X's mean to add 10. It is easy
20 to see that without converting the Roman numerals to our modern system it is difficult, if not impossible to solve 49 + 88. Subtraction, multiplication, and division with Roman numerals would be even worse.

NOTES

For the many centuries that Roman numerals were used in Europe, computation was not done with Roman numerals. It was done mechanically with a device called an abacus or another tool called the Roman counting board. These devices could be used to add or subtract numbers. Multiplication was a lot more difficult—it involved doubling numbers. For example, to compute 7×56, several steps were needed:

Step 1: Find 1 x 56	How: Write 56
Step 2: Find 2 x 56	How: Double 56 Add 56 + 56 = 112
Step 3: Find 4 x 56	How: Double 56, and then double that number Add 112 + 112 = 224
Step 4: Find 7 x 56	How: Add 1 x 56, 2 x 56, and 4 x 56 Add 56 + 112 + 224 = 392

The Origins of the Modern System

30   The modern place-value system originated in India about 1,500 years ago. Astronomers used the system, and it was used in public documents. When the Islamic empire was developing, beginning in the seventh century AD, merchants and scholars across large parts of Europe, Africa, and Asia were able to communicate with one another and exchange goods and ideas. During this time, Islamic scholars learned of the place-value system from Indian astronomers and began to spread the idea throughout the Islamic empire.

The transition to the new number system occurred differently in different places. Some cultures used the structure of the new system but changed the numerals. Some cultures adopted the Arabic numerals. The concept first spread to Eastern Arabs and then to Western Arabs in northern Africa. By the ninth century AD, Arabs in Spain were learning the Indian arithmetic.

By about 1100, Europeans gradually started using numerals to compute instead of relying on their abaci. Increasingly, trade between Europeans and Arabs helped European merchants to understand the value of the new system in the commerce that was developing. Leonardo of Pisa, a famous mathematician, wrote a book called *Liber Abaci* in the thirteenth century that popularized the new system and the use of computational algorithms to do arithmetic. By 1500, the modern decimal system was in use throughout Europe.

Other Place-Value Systems in History

The Hindu-Arabic number system is not the only number system in history that has used place value to represent numbers. Similar systems have been invented three other times in history, but the modern system has survived because it has the best features of all those systems.

The Babylonian system, which was developed about 3,000 years ago, was of base 60, which meant that each column showed a value that was 60 times the value of the place to its right. The Babylonian system had special symbols only for 1 and 10, which meant that the symbols had to be repeated in a way similar to Roman numerals.

The Mayan system, developed less than 2,000 years ago, was of base 20 and followed a pattern similar to the Babylonian system; it only had special symbols for 1 and 5. Also, the Mayan system was built to assist with time counting, so it had a quirk in one of the place values. Instead of the first three places indicating 1, 20, and 20 × 20, the third place represented 18 × 20. This created problems for computing with large numbers.

The Chinese system, from about 2,000 years ago, was a base-ten system like ours. It used a series of vertical and horizontal bars to express numbers 1 to 9, and place value was determined by the position of these symbols within a written number. Unlike these three systems, the Indian system incorporated the advantages of both the place-value structure and the use of a special symbol for each number less than 10.

The fact that three similar, but inferior, number systems have existed for thousands of years points out that the development of our modern system probably was the endpoint of a long period of struggling to represent and compute with numbers in more effective ways.

Am I on Track?

Actual Time Spent Reading

Part 1 Questions

Answer the following questions. You may refer to your reading notes, and you should cite text evidence in your responses. You will be able to refer to your answers as you write your essay in Part 2.

1 **Prose Constructed-Response** Give two important reasons why the Hindu-Arabic number system replaced other number systems. Support your response with evidence from both sources.

_____

_____

_____

_____

_____

_____

2 Which of the following sentences best presents an accurate claim one could make after reading these selections?

   a. Advancements in mathematical tools were readily accepted.

   b. The Mayan system was unique in developing special symbols.

   c. The Babylonian system is older than the Chinese system.

   d. The new number system was eventually adopted without modification.

3 Which piece of evidence best supports your answer to Question 2?

   a. "...centuries of disagreement before the modern number system was adopted throughout Europe in about AD 1500." (Source #1, lines 19–20)

   b. "...the symbols had to be repeated in a way similar to Roman numerals." (Source #2, lines 59–60)

   c. "By the ninth century AD, Arabs in Spain were learning the Indian arithmetic." (Source #2, lines 42–43)

   d. "The Chinese system, from about 2,000 years ago, was a base-ten system like ours." (Source #2, lines 67–68)

▶ Part 2 (85 minutes)

You now have 85 minutes to review your notes and sources, and to edit, draft, and revise your essay. While you may use your notes and refer to the sources, your essay must represent your original work. You may refer to your responses to Part 1 questions but you cannot change those answers. Now read your assignment and the information about how your writing will be scored; then begin your work.

Your Assignment

The deadline for the essay contest is approaching, so it is time to start writing your informative essay about number systems. Your essay should explain how number systems have changed over time. When writing your essay, find ways to use information from the two sources to support your thesis. Be sure to present your ideas in a logical order.

Informative Essay Scoring

Your essay will be scored using the following:

1. **Organization/purpose:** How well did you state your thesis and support your thesis with a logical progression of ideas? Did you use a variety of transitions between ideas? Was your focus narrow enough to lead to a well-formed conclusion?

2. **Evidence/elaboration:** How well did you incorporate relevant information from the sources? How well did you elaborate your ideas? Did you use precise language appropriate to your audience and purpose?

3. **Conventions:** How well did you follow the rules of grammar, punctuation, capitalization, and spelling?

Now begin work on your essay. Manage your time carefully so that you can:

- plan your essay, using your notes
- write your essay
- revise and edit your final draft

TASK 3

Literary Analysis

In English class, you have been assigned a literary analysis of two poems with similar themes.

First you will review a poem by Pierre de Ronsard and a poem by William Butler Yeats. After you have reviewed these sources, you will answer some questions about them. You should first skim the sources and the questions and then go back and read them carefully.

In Part 2, you will write a literary analysis in which you compare and contrast the two poems.

Time Management: Literary Analysis Task

There are two parts to most formal writing tests. Both parts of the tests are timed, so it's important to use your limited time wisely.

Part 1: Read Sources and Answer Questions

Preview the Assignment

35 minutes

You will have 35 minutes to read two poems with the same title, "When You Are Old," the first poem written by Pierre de Ronsard and the second written by William Butler Yeats. You will also answer questions about the sources.

35 minutes! That's not much time.

How Many?

How many pages of reading?

Preview the questions so you'll know which information you'll need to find as you read.

How many multiple-choice questions?

How many prose constructed-response questions?

How do you plan to use the 35 minutes?

This is a lot to do in a short time.

Estimated time to read:

    Source #1: "When You Are Old" by Pierre de Ronsard   _____ minutes

    Source #2: "When You Are Old" by William Butler Yeats   _____ minutes

Estimated time to answer questions?   _____ minutes

Total   **35 minutes**

Underline, circle, and take notes as you read. You probably won't have time to reread.

Any concerns?

_____

_____

_____

_____

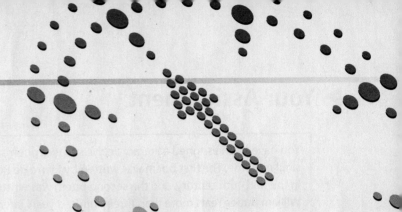

Part 2: Write the Analysis

How much time do you have? Pay attention to the clock!

Plan and Write a Literary Analysis

85 minutes

You will have 85 minutes to plan, write, revise, and edit your essay.

Your Plan

Before you start writing, decide how you will organize your literary analysis:

Point-by-Point? ☐   Subject-by-Subject? ☐

How do you plan to use the 85 minutes?

Estimated time for planning the essay?	☐ minutes
Estimated time for writing?	☐ minutes
Estimated time for editing?	☐ minutes
Estimated time for checking spelling, grammar, and punctuation?	☐ minutes
Total	**85 minutes**

Be sure to leave enough time for this step!

Notes:

_____

_____

_____

_____

_____

Reread your essay, making sure that the points are clear. Check that there are no spelling or punctuation mistakes.

▶ Your Assignment

You have been assigned a literary analysis of two poems with a similar theme. The first poem was written by Pierre de Ronsard in the mid-16th century, and the second poem was written by William Butler Yeats more than three hundred years later. You will compare and contrast the ways in which each poem treats the shared theme.

After you have reviewed both of the poems, you must answer some questions about them. Briefly skim the sources and the questions that follow. Then, go back and read each poem carefully so you will have the information you will need to answer the questions. Take notes on the sources as you read. You may refer back to your notes at any time during Part 1 or Part 2 of the performance task.

▶ Part 1 (35 minutes)

You will now read the sources. After carefully reading the sources, use the rest of the time in Part 1 to answer the five questions about them. Though your answers to these questions will help you think about what you have read and plan your literary analysis, they will also be scored as part of the test.

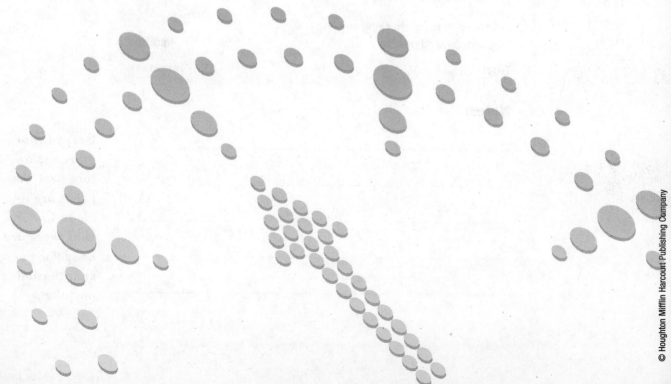

When You Are Old

by Pierre de Ronsard
translated by Andrew Lang

NOTES

When you are very old, at evening
    You'll sit and spin beside the fire, and say,
    Humming my songs, "Ah well, ah well-a-day!
When I was young, of me did Ronsard sing."
5 None of your maidens that doth hear the thing,
    Albeit with her weary task foredone,
    But wakens at my name, and calls you one
Blest, to be held in long remembering.

I shall be low beneath the earth, and laid
10 On sleep, a phantom in the myrtle shade,
    While you beside the fire, a grandame grey,
My love, your pride, remember and regret;
Ah, love me, love! we may be happy yet,
    And gather roses, while 'tis called today.

Am I on Track?

Actual Time Spent Reading

SOURCE #2:
When You Are Old

by William Butler Yeats

When you are old and gray and full of sleep,
And nodding by the fire, take down this book,
And slowly read, and dream of the soft look
Your eyes had once, and of their shadows deep;

5 How many loved your moments of glad grace,
And loved your beauty with love false or true;
But one man loved the pilgrim soul in you,
And loved the sorrows of your changing face.

And bending down beside the glowing bars
10 Murmur, a little sadly, how love fled
And paced upon the mountains overhead
And hid his face amid a crowd of stars.

Am I on Track?

Actual Time Spent Reading

Part 1 Questions

Use the remaining time to answer the questions below. Your answers to these questions will be scored. Also, they will help you think about the sources you've read, which should help you write your essay. You may refer to your notes. For Questions 1 through 4, choose the best answer. For Question 5, answer in the space provided.

1 What does the word *grandame* mean in these lines from Source #1?

> I shall be low beneath the earth, and laid
> On sleep, a phantom in the myrtle shade,
>   While you beside the fire, a grandame grey . . . "
> (lines 9–11)

   a. an elderly woman

   b. a spiritual woman

   c. an affluent woman

   d. a large woman

2 Which word or phrase from the lines of text in Question 1 best helps you understand the meaning of *grandame*?

   a. "beneath the earth"

   b. "phantom"

   c. "beside the fire"

   d. "grey"

3 Which of the following sentences best reflects the difference in the two poems' treatments of similar themes?

   a. Ronsard's poem focuses on the theme of unrequited love, while Yeats's poem focuses on the theme of love disdained.

   b. Ronsard's poem ends with the message of enjoying youth while it lasts, whereas Yeats's poem ends with the melancholy theme of lovers' regrets.

   c. Ronsard's poem includes the idea of remembrance of things past, whereas Yeats's poem contains no such message.

   d. Ronsard's poem asks the woman to view her current situation from the point of view of her future self, whereas Yeats's poem does not ask the woman to consider what her life will be like when she reaches old age.

4. Select **three** pieces of evidence from the two sources that support your answer to Question 3.

    a. "'... When I was young, of me did Ronsard sing.'" (Source #1, line 4)

    b. "Blest, to be held in long remembering." (Source #1, line 8)

    c. "I shall be low beneath the earth, and laid / On sleep, a phantom in the myrtle shade . . ." (Source #1, lines 9–10)

    d. "Ah, love me, love! we may be happy yet, / And gather roses, while 'tis called today." (Source #1, lines 13–14)

    e. "And nodding by the fire, take down this book . . ." (Source #2, line 2)

    f. "But one man loved the pilgrim soul in you . . ." (Source #2, line 7)

    g. "And bending down beside the glowing bars / Murmur, a little sadly, how love fled . . ." (Source #2, lines 9–10)

    h. "And paced upon the mountains overhead . . ." (Source #2, line 11)

5. **Prose Constructed-Response** Based on your interpretation of the two sources, write a paragraph in which you agree or disagree with this statement: "The speaker in both poems is addressing the woman he loves and imagining her as an elderly woman who is remembering a lost love." Cite specific textual evidence from both sources in your response.

_____

_____

_____

_____

_____

_____

_____

_____

_____

_____

▶ Part 2 (85 minutes)

You will have 85 minutes to review your notes and sources and plan, draft, edit, and revise your essay. While you may use your notes and refer to the sources, your essay must represent your original work. You may refer to your responses to Part 1, but you cannot change those answers. Now read your assignment and the information about how your writing will be scored; then begin your work.

Your Assignment

At this point you should begin the actual writing of your literary analysis. Think about the two poems and what you want to say about them. As you write your analysis, compare and contrast the ways the poems handle a similar theme. Make sure that you include quotations from both sources and that you present your ideas in a logical order.

Literary Analysis Scoring

Your literary analysis will be scored using the following:

1. **Organization/purpose:** How well did you state your thesis/controlling idea and support it with a logical progression of ideas? Did you use a variety of transitions between ideas? Was your controlling idea narrow enough to lead to a logical conclusion?

2. **Evidence/elaboration:** How well did you incorporate relevant information from the sources? How well did you elaborate your ideas? Did you use precise language appropriate to your audience and purpose?

3. **Conventions:** How well did you follow the rules of grammar, punctuation, capitalization, and spelling?

Now begin work on your essay. Manage your time carefully so that you can:

- plan your essay, using your notes

- write your essay

- revise and edit your final draft

Acknowledgments